The Antidote For Aphasia
The War Against Cognitive Dissonance

KAHAN TAZADAQ SHAH

Copyright © 2024 Kahan Tazadaq Shah

All rights reserved.

ISBN: 9798329671742

DEDICATION

This book is dedicated to everyone out there in the struggle of commerce and needs the Right Knowledge to endure the war of commercial warfare. There is a war waged on the mass mind, to keep the masses in debt and within a deep sleep. This book is written to give you the red pill right knowledge remedy to those who dare to read it ten times and challenge the social norms with the truth. I believe that Kahan Tazadaq has something very special to give to this world. You are about to read something very special in this book. I believe that you have something very special to give this world. Get up and get after it. Tell yourself each morning that "I am special, I am great, and I will not be ordinary." We will not be ordinary; we will be great!

Disclaimer: This scroll and pamphlet of peace is for educational purposes only and not to be construed as legal advice about what you should or should not do. The information herein is to assist you in performing your due diligence before implementing any strategy or product. This is not legal advice, I do not offer legal advice. If you need legal advice, seek a competent attorney or lawyer and please be advised. This is for educational and informational purposes only. It is protected in form and fashion, however, donations to enable us to continue our work to keep the information current and to address your specific issues are greatly appreciated. Donate at PayPal.me/ tazadaq or cash.me/$tazadaqshah or on zelle @tazadoctrine@gmail.com

Education Provides the Answers Perform Your Own Due Diligence Learn to do your own Re-search Verify Others' Research Follow the Ruach, Blaze a Trail for Those Who Follow. You Be Honorable in All Your Affairs, Kahan Tazadaq, so you know who said it
Order all of my books, DVDs and apparel at
www.kahantazadaq.net or
www.truedisciplesofchrist.org/shop
Subscribe to
(Deprogrammed Enlightener/ kahan tazadaq and in Rumble
For phone coaching email help@kahantazadaq.net or call 347-618-1783

CONTENTS

	Acknowledgments	i
1	Anger is the Fee You Pay To those who Piss You Off	1
2	A Good Lawyer Knows the Law A Great Lawyer Knows the Judges	9
3	The Father Corporation's Public Polity	30
4	Explanations of a bill of exchange	37
5	After You Sign a Mortgage Note if Falls Under UCC Article 3 Recoupment	47
6	They Are Double Entry bookkeeping	51
7	Securitization II	61
8	Rule 11	72
9	Securitization III	78
10	You Are The Creditor in Their Payables Books	86

ACKNOWLEDGMENTS

I acknowledge and bear witness that there is no God, but Yahuah and Kahan Tazadaq is his messenger

1 ANGER IS THE FEE YOU PAY TO THOSE WHO PISS YOU OFF

Anger is defined as 1: a strong feeling of displeasure and usually of antagonism (see ANTAGONISM sense 1b) 2: a threatening or violent appearance or state: RAGE sense 2

Anger isn't free, but it is a price that we pay to those that we allow to irritate us or piss us off. One of the fees that anger costs is the escalation of our blood pressure. Anger causes hypertension. If anger goes unchecked it can even lead to jail or prison.

When we allow others to drive us to not contain our emotions and react in anger, the other party is controlling our behavior due to our lack of self-control and restraint. No one is responsible for my anger but me. Likewise, no one is responsible for your anger except you. It's a decision that we make, to react angrily. People have a right to stay what they want, but we all have a choice of how we decide to respond.

If we fail to govern our affairs, then the government will step in and change us with statutory laws that we must consent to. Stop paying your advisories with anger and leasing short-term remedies, yet instead live in liberty, justice, and happiness. Anger is the price that we pay to those that we allow to control us.

King Solomon says in Proverbs 14:29 ESV
"Whoever is slow to anger has great understanding, but he who has a hasty temper exalts folly". His father David the Psalmist says in Psalm 37:8 ESV "Refrain from anger and forsake wrath! Fret not yourself; it tends only to evil". Ephesians 4:26-27 ESV "Be angry and do not sin; do not let the sun go down on your anger and give no opportunity to the devil" James 1:19 "Know this, my dear brothers and sisters: let every person be quick to listen, slow to speak, and slow to anger".

An Antidote For Aphasia

To retain control, we must begin by assessing our anger. In the book of Ephesians 4:26, Paul commands Believers to "be angry and do not sin". It is imperative to manage the emotion of anger within the bounds of righteousness. The believer is not commanded to cease from anger but to be righteous in their stewardship of anger. Unlike Yahuah, our anger is often the result of valuing the wrong things as well as being imbalanced.

1. Man's Anger is Often Rooted in Sin
"What causes fights and quarrels among you? Is it, not this, that your passions are at war within you? You desire and do not have, so you murder. You covet and cannot obtain, so you fight and quarrel" (James 4:1–2). We become angry when someone prevents us or obstructs us from our desires.

The orientation of our minds' desires re bent away from Yahuah and is directed towards the things of this world. Because of this, we are always tempted to desire other things ahead of Yahuah and his glory: the praises of men; money, comfort, and power; and inappropriate relationships. We become angry when someone prevents us from our desires. Unlike sinful anger, righteous anger is provoked by the violation of what Yahuah loves and values.

2. Unlike Yahuah, we sin in our anger because it is often disproportionate to the value of that which has been violated. Our anger seeks to convince us that we are the most important person at that moment. Therefore, those who offend us deserve the harshest punishment available.
Anger is the price you pay to those that you allow to control you. We must stop taking counsel from our anger. For many angers is a coach, the coach talks us into exploding and hurting others or imploding and hurting ourselves. We don't often equate anger with righteousness. Yahusha flipped tables in the Besorah when experiencing something known as righteous anger (Matthew 21:12). As true believers, we do have to exercise caution: there's a difference between righteous and unrighteous anger.

Righteous anger is grief over sin that arises when we witness an offense against Yah or His Word. Righteous anger doesn't seek to hurt. Love doesn't retaliate. Righteous anger stems from love because it recognizes that someone's actions or words stray from the path of righteousness. And love desires to bring someone back to the truth. The prophet Nehemiah experiences righteous anger when he discovers the abuse of poor people in his community (Nehemiah 5:6). "The wrath of Yahuah is being revealed from heaven against all the godlessness and wickedness of people, who suppress the truth by their wickedness" - Romans 1:18.

Indignation is Yah's righteous anger. Nahum 1:6 Who can stand before His indignation? Who can endure the burning of His anger? His wrath is poured out like fire And the rocks are broken up by Him.
Habakkuk 3:12 In indignation, You marched through the earth.
In anger, You trampled the nations. Zephaniah 3:8 "Therefore wait for Me," declares the Lord, "For the day when I rise as a witness. Indeed, I decide to gather nations, To assemble kingdoms, To pour out on them My indignation, All My burning anger. For all the earth will be devoured by the fire of My zeal.

Legalese
Legalese is defined as the specialized language of the legal profession. Lawyers (briefcases) and Judges (Robes (write in a manner that the common m man assumes that he comprehends but doesn't. Most people are confused by the legalese in the contracts. Words that we are taught in common parlance or colloquial speech, have different meanings in legalese. This is why Kahan Tazadaq refers to this process as aphasia.

What is aphasia?
"Aphasia is a disorder that results from damage to portions of the brain that are responsible for language. For most people, these areas are on the left side of the brain. Aphasia usually occurs suddenly, often following a stroke or head injury, but it may also develop slowly, as the result of a brain tumor or a progressive neurological disease. The disorder impairs the expression and understanding of

language as well as reading and writing. Aphasia may co-occur with speech disorders, such as dysarthria or apraxia of speech, which also result from brain damage".

The type of aphasia that modern men and women suffer is their inability to comprehend and understand words that are presented in legalese. Most people who have aphasia are middle-aged or older, but 98 percent of the world today has acquired it, including young children, because of this third type of English known as legalese. The first type of English is proper English that we are taught in English class. The second form of English is slang, and the third is legalese which only robes and briefcases comprehend.

Aphasia is caused by damage to one or more of the language areas of the brain. Most often, the cause of the brain injury is a stroke. A stroke occurs when a blood clot or a leaking or burst vessel cuts off blood flow to part of the brain. Brain cells die when they do not receive their normal supply of blood, which carries oxygen and important nutrients. Other causes of brain injury are severe blows to the head, brain tumors, gunshot wounds, brain infections, and progressive neurological disorders, such as Alzheimer's disease".

I contend there is yet another type where words are used by legalese professionals that the common man doesn't understand and signs away his substance, loses his home, and even volunteers to go to jail and prison because of his inability to comprehend contracts, that's aphasia. It's as if 98 percent of the people in society had lobotomies.

"The most common type of nonfluent aphasia is Broca's aphasia (see figure). People with Broca's aphasia have damage that primarily affects the frontal lobe of the brain. They often have right-sided weakness or paralysis of the arm and leg because the frontal lobe is also important for motor movements. People with Broca's aphasia may understand speech and know what they want to say, but they frequently speak in short phrases that are produced with great effort. They often omit small words, such as "is," "and" and "the."

Kahan Tazadaq's books are written to wake people up. It is through the ruach ha Kodesh (the holy spirit) that he speaks to you. The messenger of Yahuah spoke to me as Jeremiah; Jeremiah 1:5 "Before I formed you in the womb I knew you, before you were born, I set you apart; I appointed you as a prophet to the nations."

Remember Paul said to the Galatians in Galatians 1:15 "But when God, who set me apart from my mother's womb and called me by His grace, was pleased." Yahshayahu proclaims, Isaiah 49:1 "Listen to Me, O islands; pay attention, O distant peoples: The LORD called Me from the womb; from the body of My mother, He named Me".

Exodus 33:12,17 "And Moses said unto the LORD, See, thou sayest unto me, Bring up this people: and thou hast not let me know whom thou wilt send with me. Yet thou hast said, I know thee by name, and thou hast also found grace in my sight… So it is with Kahan Tazadaq, a man sent to you by Yah to give you this message. The Secured Creditor is not a scam it's your remedy through the blood of Yahusha(Christ). If you aren't a secured party creditor, visit www.truedisciplesofchrist.org/shop or www.kahantazadaq.net and become a secured creditor now. If you do not have all of Kahan Tazadaq's books order them now. There aren't just books they are scrolls inspired by the holy spirit to wake up the sleeping giants, which are certainly, you the people.

Kahan Tazadaq urges each reader to read each scroll ten times. Why does he suggest that? Because there are studies hat show People do NOT remember 10% of what they read, 20% of what they see, 30% of what they hear, etc.
 There is a renowned American biologist James D. Watson who once said: "The brain is the last and grandest biological frontier, the most complex thing we have yet discovered in our universe. It contains hundreds of billions of cells interlinked through trillions of connections. The brain boggles the mind."

I am grateful that wisdom has been passed down through history, from Aristotle to Pliny the Elder to Sophocles, and so forth. If you are wondering what fraction of information do we retain? This can be described as how much people remember:

10 percent of what they READ
20 percent of what they HEAR
30 percent of what they SEE
50 percent of what they SEE and HEAR
70 percent of what they SAY and WRITE
90 percent of what they DO.
Kahan Tazadaq contends that this is wisdom that learning professionals should integrate into their learning methods. Unfortunately, the complexities are intimidating. Let's make the recommendations clearer, based on our current understanding of neuroscience.

Now that you know, if you want to understand commerce and contract law, you should understand why Kahan Tazadaq suggests that you read his books and watch his videos at least ten times. Subscribe to Kahan tazadaq on YouTube. Google Tazadaq and you will be astounded by what you thought you knew. This book is one of many that you must read ten times. This is a revolution of your mind, "complete constructive change. This book is inspired by the Ruach ha Kodesh. It is by the grace of yah that I give you this message.

This book is also a call to return to Yah/God's will of male patriarchy. Today's women refuse to play their roles as wives and mothers. Masculinity and leaders are a woman warring against the nature in which she was created. Feminism is a germ that must be uprooted to save the world. Too many women are looking for heaven in hell. What will it take to wake us up? It takes us being able to accept the truth and apply it. This book is the truth. Stop taking counsel from your ignorance and lies.

An Antidote For Aphasia

An Antidote For Aphasia

Order now @ www.kahantazadaq.net

2 A GOOD LAWYER KNOWS THE LAW A GREAT LAWYER KNOWS THE JUDGES

This is my reality for the remainder of my life. What's yours? Unless you continue to work on your craft each day, it's where you are now. Average. You had better realize to be legendary, that pain is necessary, and difficulty is essential. You have greatness within you, and now is your opportunity to bring it out.

Bankers and lawyers control the world. Some of you reading this book right now are at the bottom. Young king the best gifts come from the bottom. The rose grew through the concrete and so can you. Henceforth hold the dictators accountable for the deception that they have manipulated us with. You hold your head low, but your dreams don't; live down there. The British Legal System is Of mixed Common And Roman Law. This system has been used to enslave The USA and the world. BAR stands for British Accreditation Registry. These public servants don't have a license to practice law, they have BAR cards. The reason folks can be changed by practicing laws without a license is due to copyright violations.

Any robe (Judge), government agent, or bureaucrat who has sworn to uphold the Constitution for the United States - who is violating that oath - is Guilty of Treason. The Penalty is still DEATH BY HANGING.

Post-Revolutionary War of 1776
Post Revolutionary War of 1776, since no actual surrender papers had been signed, King George III decided that the colonies still belonged to him, to England, and all that remained was for him to figure out how to get them back again under his direct control. To do this he determined to use the banks, both United States and England, as one method. But to underpin his efforts, he needed briefcases (lawyers) or attorneys here in the 'colonies' to make it all happen. The 'legal' ramifications of how things had to be brought about had become an important issue to England ever since the days of the Magna Carta.

An Antidote For Aphasia

Briefcases, known more prominently as "Barristers", had arisen to great power in England since the days of the old knights. But the battle by these heirs of knighthood this time was forged against good and not evil, for this new thing that the People in America were labeling "freedom" was a dangerous consideration for a King.

King George needed the briefcases or attorneys over in the Colonies to be members, or Esquires, of England's International Bar Association, the only Bar association in the world, headquartered right in good old London town and under his direct control, but with operations established in the United States, with certain strong ties into the Congress. The International Bar Association was alive and well in America.

That thing called "Freedom" would soon come to an end. Therefore, King George's knowing the law is foundational for any lawyer. It involves understanding statutes, regulations, and legal precedents relevant to a case. This knowledge forms the basis for building arguments, advising clients, and navigating the complexities of legal proceedings.

However, knowing the Robes (judges) goes beyond statutory law. It refers to understanding the personalities, tendencies, and preferences of the robes who preside over cases. Different robes may have distinct approaches to interpreting the law, applying legal principles, and managing courtroom proceedings. A great briefcase can anticipate how a robe might respond to certain arguments, tailor their approach accordingly, and effectively advocate for their client's position based on this understanding.

In essence, while both aspects — knowing the law and knowing the robes are crucial for a successful legal practice, the latter often sets apart exceptional lawyers who can strategically navigate the human element of the judiciary system.

The Bar was England's own British Accreditation Registry, its members were nobles - being above the common person, and all briefcases or attorneys had to belong to it, and they were under the will of the King, and the Bank of England. And if there was any opposition to his plan, he might just cause another WAR to maintain his position for control of the United States.

Speeding forward we can consider an interesting legal issue. According to this and many other sources, there was a 13th Amendment to the Constitution for the United States of America -- not the one that we assume that
have now. The previous 13th Amendment was removed during the time just before or during the Civil War. Kahan Tazadaq discovered that in the winter of 1983, archival research expert David Dodge, and former Baltimore police investigator Tom Dunn were searching for evidence of government corruption in public records stored in the Belfast Library on the coast of Maine. By the grace of Yahuah, they discovered the library's oldest authentic copy of the Constitution for the United States (printed in 1825). Both men were stunned to see this document included a 13th Amendment that no longer appears on current copies of the Constitution.

There is a reason that this is kept out of public view. The Amendment's language historical context and principal intent of this 'missing' 13th Amendment was to prohibit lawyers, and any members of the Bar Association, from serving in government! Our government!

This missing 13th Amendment suppressed and even stopped the forming or continued existence of any Bar association for over four decades, from 1822 to 1867, and evidence of its existence has been found in over 10 different states and territories throughout the United States. How did a lawfully ratified Amendment to the Constitution of the United States simply disappear, vanish, without so much as a nod of disturbance or at least some curiosity from the American people? Why isn't this taught in school? Why aren't the things that Khan Tazadaq teaches not taught in school?

Why is it that the Amendment which deliberately targeted attorneys who were members of the Bar Association, was removed?

It intended to prevent Bar members from holding any public office -

thereby preventing attorneys from passing legislation that would most assuredly serve the greedy and nefarious interests of not only the Bar Association itself but also the King of England, right along with the other royal heads of Europe? So that we the people might not be conquered from within as opposed to without?

The Color game is for slaves:

The courts only recognize TWO classes of people in the United States today

Debtors And Creditors. Not black, not white, not Asian or Hispanic. If you are playing the color game, and are a racist, then you are a DEBTOR slave.

The concept and status of DEBTORS and creditors are very important for you to comprehend. Every legal action where you are brought before the court (e.g. traffic ticket, murder, property dispute or permits, income tax, credit cards, bank loans, or anything else they might dream up to charge you where you find yourself in front of a court) - IT IS AN EQUITY COURT, administering commercial law having a debtor/creditor law as the controlling law. Today, we have an equity court, but not an equity court as referred to in the Constitution of the U.S., or any of the legal documents before 1938.

All the courts have been changed, starting with the Supreme Court decision of 1938 in Erie R.R. v. Thompkins, 304 U.S 64 (1938). That case gives you the background that led to this decision.

When Kahan Tazadaq was researching he couldn't find a definition for legislative democracy. It bothered him. However, by researching more, Kahan began to see the fraud that is being perpetrated on all of us Americans.

Please understand that this fraud is a 24-hour, 7 days a week, year after year continuous fraud. It doesn't happen just occasionally. This fraud is constantly upon you all your life. Whether you are aware of it or not, this fraud is perpetually and incessantly upon you and your family.

When the U.S. Inc. Went To Geneva - 1930's

For you to understand just how this fraud works, you need to know the history of its inception. It goes like this: from 1928 to 1932 there were five years of Geneva conventions. The nations of the world met in Geneva, Switzerland for 5 continuous years to set up what would be the policy of all the participating countries. During the year 1930 the U.S., Great Britain, France, Germany, Italy, Spain, Portugal, etc., all declared bankruptcy. If you try to look up the 1930 minutes, you will not find them because they don't publish this volume.

If you try to find the 1930 volume which contains the minutes of what happened, you will probably not find it. This volume has been pulled out of circulation or is hidden in the library and is very hard to find. This volume contains the evidence of the bankruptcy.

Going into 1932, they stopped meeting in Geneva. In 1932 Franklin D. Roosevelt came into power as President of the United States. Roosevelt's job was to put into place and administer the bankruptcy that had been declared two years earlier. The corporate government needed a key Supreme Court decision. The corporate United States government had to have a legal case on the books to set the stage for recognizing, implementing, and supporting the bankruptcy.

Now, this doesn't mean the bankruptcy wasn't implemented before 1938 with the Erie RR v. Thompkins decision. The bankruptcy started in 1930-1931. The bankruptcy started when Roosevelt came into office. He was sworn in in January 1933. He started right away in bankruptcy with what is known as the " Banking Holiday" and proceeded to pull all gold coins out of circulation. That was the beginning of the United States' Public Policy for bankruptcy.

How F.D. Roosevelt Stacks Supreme Court

It is a known historical fact that during 1933 and 1937-1938, there was a big fight between Roosevelt and the Supreme Court Justices. Roosevelt tried to stack the Supreme Court with a bunch of his pals. Roosevelt tried to enlarge the number of Justices and he tried to change the slant of the Justices. The corporate United States had to have one Supreme Court case that would support its bankruptcy problem.

There was resistance to Roosevelt's court-stacking efforts. Some of the Justices tried to warn us that Roosevelt was tampering with the law and with the courts. Roosevelt was trying to see to it that prior decisions of the court were overturned. He was trying to bring in a new order, a new procedure for the law of the land.

The "Father Corporation" Goes Bankrupt

A bankruptcy case was needed on the books to legitimize the fact that the corporate U.S. had already declared bankruptcy! This bankruptcy was effectuated by a compact that the corporate states had with the corporate government (Corporate Capitol of the several corporate states). This compact tied the corporate several states to corporate Washington, D.C. (the headquarters of the corporation called "The United States"). Since the United States Corporation, having established its headquarters within the District of Columbia, declared itself to be in a state of bankruptcy, it automatically declared bankruptcy for all its subsidiaries who were effectively connected corporate members (who happened to be the corporate state governments of the Union). The corporate state governments didn't have to vote on bankruptcy.

The bankruptcy automatically became effective because of a Compact/Agreement between each of the
corporate state governments and

THE FATHERS CORPORATION.

(Note: The writer has taken the liberty of using the term "Father Corporation" to communicate the interconnected power of the corporate Federal government relative to her associated corporate States. It is Kahan Tazadaq's understanding that the States created the Federal Government, however, for all practical purposes, the Federal Government has taken control of her
"Creators", the States.) She has become a beast out of control for power. She has for her trade names the following: "United States", "U.S.", "U.S.A.", "United States of America", Washington, D.C., District of Columbia, Feds, Federal Government.

It has its own U.S. Army, Navy, Air Force, Marines, Parks, Post Office, etc., etc., etc. Because she is claiming to be bankrupt, she freely gives her land, her personnel, and the money she steals from the Americans via the I.R.S. and her state corporations, to the United Nations and the International Bankers as payment for her debt. The UN and the International Bankers use this money and services for various worldwide "projects", which include war. War is an extremely lucrative business for the bankers of the New World Order. Loans for destruction. Loans for re-construction. Loans for controlling people on her world property.

U.S. Inc. Declares Bankruptcy The corporate U.S., then, is the head corporate member, who met in Geneva, to decide for all its corporate body members. The corporate representatives of several states were not in attendance. If the states had the power to declare bankruptcy regardless of whether Washington D.C. declared bankruptcy or not, then the several states would have been represented at Geneva.

Several states of America were not represented. Consequently, whatever Washington D.C. agreed to at Geneva was passed on automatically, via compact to the several corporate states as a group, association, corporation, or club member, they all agreed and declared bankruptcy as one government corporate group in 1938.

The several states only needed a representative in Geneva by way of the U.S. in Washington, D.C. The delegates of the corporate United States attended the meetings and spoke for several corporate states as well as for the
mother corporation located in Washington, D.C., the seat and headquarters of the Federal Corporate Government. And presto, BANKRUPTCY was declared for all!

From 1930 to 1938, the states could not enact any law or decide any case that would go against the Federal
Government. The case had to come down from the Federal level so that the states would rely on the Federal
decision and use this decision as justification for the bankruptcy

process within the states.

Emergence of the UCC as Law of the Land

By 1938, the corporate Federal Government had the true bankruptcy case they had been looking for. Now, the bankruptcy that had been declared back in 1930 could be upheld and administered. That's why the Supreme Court had to be stacked and made corrupt from within. The new players on the Supreme Court fully understood that they had to destroy all other case law that had been established before 1938.

The Federal Government had to have a case to destroy all precedence, all appearance, and even the statute of law itself. That is, the Statutes at Large had to be perverted. They finally got their case in Erie R.R. v. Thompkins. It was right after that case that the American Law Institute and the National Conference of Commissioners on Uniform State Laws listed right in the front of the Uniform Commercial Code, began creating the Uniform Commercial Code that is on our backs today. Let us quote directly from the preface of the 1990 Official Text of the Uniform Commercial Code, 12th edition.

The Code was originally approved by its sponsors and the American Bar Association in 1952 and was revised in 1958 to incorporate several changes that had been recommended by the New York Law Revision Commission and other agencies. Subsequent amendments that were deemed desirable in the light of experience under the Code were approved by the Permanent Editorial Board in 1962 and 1966.

The groups and associations of private lawyers got together and started working on the
Uniform Commercial Code (UCC). It was somewhere between 1930 and 1940, I don't recall, but by the early 40's and during the war, this committee was working to form the UCC and got it ready to put on the market.
The UCC is the law merchant's code for the administration of bankruptcy. The UCC is now the new law of the land, as far as the

courts are concerned.

This Legal Committee of lawyers put everything, Negotiable Instruments, Security, Sales, Contracts & Agreements, and the whole mess under the UCC.

That's where the "Uniform" word comes from. It means it was uniform from state to state, as well as being uniform within the District of Columbia. It doesn't mean you didn't have the uniform instrument laws on the books before this time. It means the laws were not uniform from state to state. By the middle 1960's, every state had passed the UCC into law. The states had no choice but to adopt the newly formed Uniform Commercial Code as the law of the land. The states fully understood they had to administrate bankruptcy.

Washington D.C. adopted the Uniform Commercial Code in 1963, just six weeks or so after Kennedy was killed.

Your Briefcase 's (Lawyer's) Secret Oath
What was the effect and the significance of the Erie RR. v. Thompkins case decision of 1938? The significance is that since the Erie decision, no cases are allowed to be cited that are before 1939. There can be no mixing of the old law with the new law.

The lawyers (who were members of the American Bar Association and were and are currently under and controlled by the Lawyer's Guild of Great Britain) created, formed, and implemented the new bankruptcy law. The American Bar Association is a franchise of the Lawyers Guild of Great Britain. Since the Erie RR. v. Thompkins case was decided; the practice of law in this country was never again to be the same.

It has been reported (source unknown to the writer) that every lawyer in existence and every lawyer coming up must take a SECRET OATH to support the bankruptcy. This seems to make sense after reading about

Mr. Sweet's CASE FILE DISAPPEARANCE is discussed below. There is more to it. Not only do they promise to support the

bankruptcy, but the lawyers and judges also promise never to reveal who the true creditor party is in the bankruptcy proceedings! In court, there is
never identification and appearance of the true character and principle of the proceedings. This is where you can get them for not making an appearance in court. If there is no appearance of the true party to the
action, then there is no way the defendant can know the true NATURE AND CAUSE OF THE ACTION.

You are never told the true NATURE AND THE CAUSE OF WHY YOU ARE IN FRONT OF THEIR COURT.
The court is forbidden to tell you that information. That's why, if you question the true nature and cause, the judge will say, "It's not my job to tell you. You are not retaining me as an attorney, and I can't give you
legal advice from the bench. I suggest you hire a lawyer."

What about Practicing Law Without A License?
Lawyer - Learned in the law to advise in a court
Barrister - One who is privileged to plead at the bar
Advocate - One who pleads within the BAR for a defendant
Attorney - One who transfers or assigns, within the bar, another's money, goods/ property, rights, and title
to and acting on behalf of the ruling crown (government).

If anyone ever charges you with illegal/unlawful "Practicing law without a license", just say: "No attorney or lawyer in the U.S. has ever been "LICENSED" to practice law" (they've exempted themselves, and no such crime exists) as they are abstract, artificial, bogus, bullshit, counterfeit, dead, fraudulent, imaginary, non-existent, statutory "FICTION OF LAW" "person" and only an "ADMITTED MEMBER" to practice law in
the private franchise member "club" called the "BAR" (British or BARrister Aristocratic Regency, or British Accreditation Registry -- B.A.R. as input in Jail Behind BARs, to BAR = stop = arrest = kidnap = abduct, or
also, attorneys are absolute "BAR" red from challenging the

jurisdiction of the court), and as such they are unlawful "un-registered foreign agents". Attorneys and lawyers only have "BAR Cards" which are clearly
not "licenses.

The lawyers, who are members of one or more of the 50 State Bar Associations (private membership clubs), which are franchised by the American Bar Association (A.B.A.), are all under and controlled by the
Lawyers Guild of Great Britain which created, formed, and implemented the U.S. financial BANKRUPTCY law filed 3/9/33, which bankruptcy is still in full force and effect today, for and on behalf of the International Banksters as "Creditors" thereof. Therefore, said attorneys/lawyers are Traitors, Esquires (noblemen training for knighthood, Un-Constitutional title of honor and nobility = Esquires), alien and foreign "non-citizens" and are specifically prohibited by the USA Constitution from ever voting in any election (Election Fraud) or from ever holding any elected public office of trust whatsoever! Even "jailhouse lawyer" prisoner inmates are Constitutionally protected and assured access to the courts. Attorneys are not lawyers, as attorneys practice "attornment" (turn over goods, services, etc. to another i.e. robbers and thieves) and lawyers practice "law". Lawyers are supposedly learned in the law
and advise in a court while an attorney transfers or assigns someone's rights or property, etc to another and acts on behalf of the ruling crown (government). In 1878 the American legal system came under the control of a Labor Union known as the Worldwide (BRITISH) BAR ASSOCIATION. Consequently, "their" courts have become "Closed Union Shops".

The judges have become the union bosses of those "private" for-profit courts. These judges are overseen by a principal union boss or union superintendent, a Supreme Court Justice of the State. The criminal attorneys, barristers, and counselors at law, and lawyers, together with the international banksters, control everything of importance in government (they unlawfully control, own, and have usurped (by force of law) all 3 branches of government), the Bar Association controls the Attorneys, et al, and the aristocratic elite monied power control the worldwide franchised "private" British Bar Associations (the American Bar Association is but one private franchise among hundreds worldwide).

The Bar Association Labor Union

The Bar Association Labor Union only allows union lawyers called attorneys to use the publicly tax-financed "private" courts (Union Hall or Local Union) with Local Rules called "Rules of the Court". The ultimate goal of the BAR Association is the overthrow the GOVERNMENT of the United States and its Constitution, the complete and total enslavement and subjugation of its people, and to re-establish an absolute incontestable form of ancient Babylonian and Masonic Medieval British Feudalism in America and the rest of the world which will become the New World Order, One World Government, under Mob Rule "Democracy" (the merging of capitalism and communism, and a "military Dictatorship run by the "Commander-in-Chief" called the "President").

Attorneys first came into existence because GOVERNMENT-created and invented abstract, artificial, bogus, counterfeit, dead, fraudulent, non-existent statutory "FICTIONS OF LAW" "persons", "citizens", "individuals", "people", the "public", "res-idents" (the thing, identified), "taxpayers", "registered voters", etc. could not (re)present themselves in court since they did not really exist and so could not speak for themselves and thus need a "spokesperson". Therefore, they had to have a mouthpiece [someone to speak for and on their behalf and to "DE-fend" (NOT fend, NOT ward off, not fight for NOR offer defense) them] to speak for and "RE-present" (RE-create, RE-fashion, RE-form, RE-make, RE-mold, RE-place, RE-produce,
change, convert, exchange, substitute and TRANCEform) these non-existent brainless, deaf and dumb fictions. Back then as now, living and breathing souls, real and natural, flesh and blood "men or women" as defendants in court could not be re-presented by a third party since they could and were required to speak for themselves. A "human being" does not have a right to re-presentation, he has a right to "assistance of counsel". These are two very different

concepts.

Pro Se status
Pro Se status is nothing more than the de-fendant moving the court to allow him to waive the right to "assistance of counsel". The word "attorney" (attorn-ee, attorn-ey) definition derives from "to attorn" meaning "to turn over, to transfer to another money, goods/property, rights or title". In other words, lawyers are simply highly paid criminals, embezzlers, leeches (blood suckers), magots, parasites, prostitutes (who persecute and prosecute), robbers and thieves, etc., hired to rob and steal from Peter (the plaintiff
and the defendant) to pay Paul, Paul being the British Aristocratic Monarchy which franchises the worldwide BAR associations, the creditors of the U.S. bankruptcy of 3/9/33, and the international banksters.

The true Creditor would have to say "It's a bankruptcy proceeding" and "I'm the Creditor and the DEFENDANT is the DEBTOR." In all court cases where the GOVERNMENT is the alleged plaintiff, ninety-four percent (94 %) of all private DEFENDANTS are summarily found "guilty". Today, we are again enslaved. Private natural American people have been deceived, lied to, set up and tricked into carrying the U.S. Inc. perpetual corporate debt under bankruptcy laws.

Every time Americans appear in their private for-profit courts, the corporate U.S. bankruptcy is being administrated against them without their knowledge and lawful consent. That is criminal FRAUD in the highest order and fraud is internationally exempt from any "Statute of Limitations". All corporate
bankruptcy administration is done by "Public Policy" of, by, and for the Mother/Parent Corporation (U.S. INC.). Lawyers and judges also swear secret (un-constitutional) satanic (kol nidre)/masonic oaths, which oaths have always dis-favored the plaintiff and the DEFENDANT, and which secret oaths swear total allegiance to either ancient dark secret societies, the worldwide BAR Association(s) originating and franchised out of Britain, and/or the state (ie, fiction "GOVERNMENT"). Such oaths are in direct

conflict with the attorney's presumed fiduciary capacity, duty, relationship, and responsibility to his client, the plaintiff or the DEFENDANT (those who hired and paid him), his sworn loyalty, confidence, dedication, good faith, trust and representation already having been previously given, pledged and sworn to his masters and handlers, and as such, it is absolutely impossible for any admitted member of the BAR to re-present (recreate, re-form, re-package and TRANCEform a real live soul/man into a fiction STRAW MAN) any client in honesty and truth, and are simply high paid legal prostitutes.

The false argument and rebuttable presumption that attorneys are "licensed" when they are sworn in by the presiding judge of the STATE or the U.S. Supreme Court and issued a "Bar Card" is pure bullshit hogwash. Since when can an officer of a private CORPORATION, the "administrative non-judicial" Court, not legally different than McDonald's CORPORATION, Federal Reserve CORPORATION, or Federal Express CORPORATION - swear in or license anybody? Anyone who "affirms or swears under oath" with or without your (right) hand on a bible or raised up in the air is specifically prohibited, estopped, ab initio, from so doing in Matthew 5:33-37 (" ... Do not swear at all ...") and James 5:12 ("But above all, my brethren,
do not swear, either by heaven or by the earth, or with any other oath. But let your "yes" be "yes" and your "no" be "no", lest you fall into Judgement"). Generally, judges must be attorneys first and foremost because
that tends to ensure that the judge has been properly brainwashed, conditioned, indoctrinated, programmed, and trained by the GOVERNMENT's" law schools and peers.

Any and every lawyer, judge, or court system is your "SWORN ENEMY" affording you NO "Full Disclosure" of all material facts, NO "Equal Protection" of/under the laws NOR "Due Process" of law, and they are NOT your advocates seeking fair play, equity and justice for the real you. When you accept a GOVERNMENT
court-appointed defense attorn-ey or you hire your attorn-ey you have then contracted with a "third party agent" to act for and on your

behalf to "re-"present (transform) you, and you have just given that criminal attorney your "Power of Attorney".

The original "missing" (stolen, removed, and replaced) Thirteenth Amendment to the Constitution of the United States reads as follows: "If any citizen of the United States shall accept, claim, receive, or retain any title of nobility or honor (all attorn-eys have accepted the alien/foreign title and honor of "Esquire, Esq." or knighthood), or shall without the consent of
Congress, accept and retain any present, pension, office, or emolument of any kind whatever, from any emperor, king, prince (aristocracy), or foreign power, such person shall cease to be a citizen of the United States, and shall be incapable of holding any office of trust or profit under them, or either of them." -- (Words in parenthesis are mine).

Are Attorneys Lawyers?
In the U.S., they're collectively called everything from "attorney" to "lawyer" to "counselor." Are these terms truly equivalent, or has the identity of one been mistaken for another? What exactly is a "Licensed BAR Attorney"? This credential accompanies every legal paper produced by attorneys - along with a State Bar License number.

As we are about to show you, an `attorney' is not a `lawyer', yet the average American improperly interchanges these words as if they represent the same occupation, and the average American attorney unduly accepts the ho nor of being called "lawyer" when he is not. To discern the difference, and where we stand within the current court system, it's necessary to examine the British origins of our U.S. courts and the terminology that has been established from the beginning. It's important to understand the proper lawful definitions for the various titles we now give these court-related occupations. The legal profession in the U.S. is directly derived from the British system. Even the word "bar" is of British origin: BAR.

A particular portion of a courtroom. Named from the space

enclosed by two bars or rails: one of which separated the judge's bench from the rest of the room; the other shut off both the bench and the area for lawyers engaged in trials from the space allotted to suitors, witnesses, and others. Such people who appeared as speakers (advocates, or counsel) before the court, were said to be "called to the bar", that is, privileged so to appear, speak and otherwise serve in the presence of the judges as "barristers". The corresponding phrase in the United States is "admitted to the bar". -A Dictionary of Law (1893).

A 1996 article that still applies... Neither law nor elected representatives govern America. Our nation is controlled and manipulated by a committee of lawyers, the American Bar (fly) Association, the infamous Bar(flies), who care not about us but about themselves and their wealth. In September 1995, for the first time in American history, the inflow of tax revenues was less than our government had paid on just the interest it owed. In other words, our Federal government can't even pay the interest on the loans they've promised to pay to mostly foreign entities. So, we decided to dig deeper into how this came about. What we uncovered is shocking, to say the very least. It seems that the crafty powers that control this great land behind the scenes are about to choke us into submission. The United States, Incorporated declared bankruptcy, once again, in 1933. President Franklin D. Roosevelt, the author of American socialism, declared this in Executive Orders 6073, 6102, 6111, and 6260. At the same time, all gold and silver were taken away from We the People. This was done under the Trading with the Enemy Act of October 6, 1917, when our entire nation was placed under an economic "emergency". Incidentally, this "emergency" has never been rescinded and we are still subject to the same "emergency" declaration today.

To bail out our insolvent federal government, the several incorporated franchise States of the Union pledged the faith and credit of We the People to the National Government. This is how we ended up with the Social Security Administration and the Council of State Governments, among many other socialistic entities. On January 22, 1937, these organizations published their Declaration of

INTERdependence in The Book of States where they openly declared that all farmers (land owners) were no more than feudal tenants (page 155, 1937 edition).

This was, and still is, the method used to steal private property from We the People to benefit others, without just compensation. Today, a homeowner doesn't receive a lawful deed or title to his land. Instead, he receives a Warranty Deed whereby the State holds the actual title and deed as collateral for the National government's debt (the corporate body known as the United States located in Washington City). You don't own your land... the United States does.

The same applies to motor vehicles. You are given a Certificate of Title when you buy a car, but the actual title itself is being held as collateral by the government. You are holding a piece of paper that certifies that the title exists. In other words, even if you have no house mortgage or car loan, you still do not *own* them ... the United States holds title to *your* private property! The previously mentioned Council of State Governments is now the National Conference Of Commissioners On Uniform State Laws. This organization's membership consists of only Bar(fly) licensed lawyers, the illegal and immoral monopoly that controls our nation. These licensed socialists (communists seize private land without compensation, don't they?) parade around with the royal Nobility Title of Esquire (Esq.), but according to the Constitution And By-Laws of their organization, they lobby for, pass, order, and execute statutory provisions to "help implement international treaties of the United States or where world uniformity would be desirable"

Source-1990/91 Reference Book, National Council of Commissioners
On Uniform State Laws, page 2.

The ABA LIE: Unauthorized Practice of Law. Just how does a Good and Lawful Christian defend Himself when forced, against His Will, to stand and speak before the purported 'courts' now operating in the United States? Is He to be mute and say nothing, citing the Laws of God? Although every

Christian has the Right to choose His
court, this is not so practical when he is forced by duress and coercion to 'appear' in a court He has not chosen nor recognized as being subject to God's Laws.

How can he 'appear' in an un-Godly court? Our answer to this is to do as Yahusha did when He was forced to stand before the judgment of the un-Godly. There is no set of Rules other than the example His Word has already laid out for Us. However, every believer should know how this world operates, and that includes the purported 'laws' and 'courts' being forced upon us over and above God's Sovereign Laws.

To defend oneself is nearly impossible in their 'courts', and to seek the assistance of Godly counsel is not allowed by what they dare to call, but refuse to define, as the "unauthorized practice of law". There may be much truth to the claim that the Fourteenth Amendment to the federal constitution was instigated by the legal professionals' trade union, now known as The American Bar Association.

Many facts support the claim that this "Bar" monopoly was established in Christian America, immediately after Lincoln's (un)Civil War, to create and substitute a 'colorless' system of uniformed general slavery to replace the previous system of black slavery. This was to have been implemented by guaranteeing a monopoly of the courts for their member attorneys, judges, and Municipal Corporations (City, County, and State). This monopolizing and unlawful labor union, The Bar Association, has forbidden anyone but their exclusive member attorneys to give legal advice or representation, which has prevented any Good and Lawful Christian from being assisted in these purported 'Courts of Law' by a non-union lawyer or by a "nonlawyer", as used in their terminology.

U.S. Corp is Distinct and Separate From PRIVATE americans

"We the People" who created and signed the

contract/compact/agreement of, by, and for the Constitutional Corporation (U.S.); using the trade name of the "United States of America", is a corporate entity (legal fiction) which is DISTINCT AND SEPARATE from Americans or the unenfranchised people of America. The private natural American people did not create the corporation of the United States. The United States Inc. did not create the private natural American people.

America and americans were in existence before the creation of the United States Corporation. The United States Corporation has located its U.S. headquarters in Washington, D.C. Virginia state (state territory) gave land to the newly formed United States Corporation. Notice, that here, we have a state giving something of value (land) to the United States.

The United States Corporation agreed in the Constitutional contract, to protect the states. Instead, because of their bankruptcy (Corporate U.S. Bankruptcy) this U.S. corporation has enslaved the states and the people by deception, and at the will of their foreign banksters, with whom they have been doing business. Our forefathers gave their lives and property to prevent enslavement.

Today, we are once again enslaved. Private natural American people have been tricked, deceived, and set up to carry U.S. Inc.'s perpetual corporate debt under bankruptcy laws. Every time Americans appear in court, corporate U.S. bankruptcy is being administered against them, without their knowledge and lawful consent. That is FRAUD! All corporate bankruptcy administration is done by "Public Policy" - of by and for the Mother Corporation (U.S. Inc.).

The American Dream, Where did it go?

An Antidote For Aphasia

An Antidote For Aphasia

3 THE FATHER CORPORATION'S "PUBLIC POLICY"

Most people go about life living a lie that is told to them and by them. They are too daunted to run towards their dreams. What's your dream? What are you willing to do that you have never done before? What are you willing to say that you have never said before? Kahan Tazadaq started with nothing. But he was willing to rise. He had nothing and that was everything that he needed. My dreams were bigger than my disappointment. What if you are not the only one that wants what you want? You must outwork them, or they will steal your dream. Ask yourself, "Can I do this?' Can I be successful as a secured creditor? What is that person who left you or gave up on you as an opportunity to be great?
Do what you hate to be great! Are you going to complain in the face of difficulty or seize the opportunity?

Corporate bankruptcy is carried out under the corporate public policy of the corporate Federal Government in corporate Washington, D.C. The states use state public policy to carry out the Federal public policy of Washington D.C. Public Policy and only public policy is being administered against you in the corporate courts today.

The public policy that is dictated by all the courts, from the smallest to the most powerful courts in the world, is public policy. This is why, when people like us go to court without being represented by a lawyer, we throw a monkey wrench into the corporate administrative proceedings. Why? Because all public policy corporate lawyers are pledged to uphold public policy, which is the corporate U.S. administration of their corporate bankruptcy.

That is why you will find stamped on many, if not all of our briefs, When we go in to defend ourselves or file a claim, we're not supporting the corporate bankruptcy administration and procedure. The arguments we put forth pre-date 1938. We come in with Constitutional law, etc. All these early cases support our right not to be in bankruptcy. However, the corporate court, lawyers, and judges have promised to give no judicial recognition of any case "before 1938". Before 1938, the law was not a public policy law. All these old cases were not public law-deciding cases. Today, the cases are all decided under corporate public policy. The public policy exists to administer bankruptcy for the benefit of the bankster creditors and to protect the bankster creditors. Corporate public policy can allow the creditor to say to the corporate legislatures, "I want a law passed requiring my debtors to wear seat belts. Why? Because I want to be able to milk my debtors for the longest period possible." It doesn't behoove the creditor to allow all his labor-producing debtors to die at an average age of 30 years.

The Real Estate Trap
How do they work this scheme around real estate? These bankster creeps have agreed that it is corporate public policy, that all land (property) be pledged to the creditor to satisfy the debt of the bankruptcy, which the creditor claims under bankruptcy.

They get away with this the same way that they get away with any other case that is brought before the court, whether it is a traffic ticket, IRS, or whatever. Here is how it works. You have signed instruments giving information and jurisdiction to the banksters through their agents. The instruments (forms) you signed include, but are not limited to the following: social security registration, use of the social security number, IRS forms, driver's license, traffic citation, jury duty, voter registration, using their address, zip code, U.S. postal service, a deed, a mortgage application, etc. etc.

The banksters then use that instrument (document) under the Uniform Commercial Code (UCC) as a contract/agreement. These documents are considered promissory contracts where you promise to perform. This scheme involves you, without you ever becoming directly in contact or contract with the true creditor.

What's more, you are never informed as to whom the true creditor is and it is never divulged to you the true nature and the true cause of the paperwork that you are filling out. If you examine your real estate deed, you will find that you promised to pay taxes to the corporate government. On the property you originally acquired through a mortgage, you will notice that the bank never promised to pay taxes. You did. The corporate government at all levels never promised to pay taxes to the creditor. You did. In tax and collection problems relating to real estate being enforced against you, you will notice that there is no mention in the mortgage or the deed stating the true nature and cause of the action. Since you made the promise to perform, you get a bill every year for property taxes.

You don't realize that the only way they can bill you for taxes is through your stupidity of AGREEING to pay the tax. You volunteered. They took advantage of you, conning you to promise to pay property taxes. When they send you their bill, they are coming against you for the collection of the promise you made to the creditor. Now the creditor on the paperwork appears to be the local bank. The bank has loaned you credit.

The bank hasn't loaned you anything. It was not their credit to loan. This is why the bank can't loan credit. There is credit involved, but not the bank's credit. It is the credit of the International banksters. The international banksters are making you the loan based upon their operation of bankruptcy claim which they presume to have against you personally as well as your property. Now, let's say you are not aware of the remedies provided for you within the Uniform Commercial Code (UCC). The UCC provides or allows you to dishonor the county's presentment of the tax bill.

You don't pay your tax bill. You therefore just sit on it and don't do or say anything. A couple of years go by and suddenly you are being sent letters to pay up what is owed or else in a certain period your property will be taken from you and put up for a tax sale. Now here is what is interesting - If you don't pay your tax bill, and they contact you asking you to pay it and you don't pay it, they will declare you in default. It is based on that default as provided in the UCC that they sell your property for the tax (rent).

However, the county never goes to court to put into the record the identification of the real creditor. The county does not state the true nature and cause of the action against you (a bankruptcy action disguised as a tax action). Why? Because, under bankruptcy implementation, they have developed a legal procedure that is based upon YOUR PROMISE TO PAY. The procedure provides that they don't have to come to court to get a court order authorizing the sale of their property.

Therefore, the real creditor never makes an appearance in court. The reality is, that you are denied any possibility of appearing in court to exercise your right to challenge the creditor. To ask if he became a creditor under "public policy". To ask if it is under "public policy", just what is "public policy"? And how did you (as an international banker) become a "creditor" to me and everyone else in this country (American people)?

They don't want you to ask the real creditor (the International Banksters), to PRODUCE THE DOCUMENTS upon which your debt is established. If they were forced to go into court, they would have to produce the deed or mortgage showing you KNOWINGLY, WILLINGLY, and VOLUNTARILY promised to pay the corporate public debt. You did not KNOWINGLY, WILLINGLY, and VOLUNTARILY promise to pay any U.S. Corporate Bankruptcy obligation made in the 1930's. This would, of course, expose their racket.

The fact is that there was no debt connected to you until you agreed to it through their deception and fraud. The deception, in a broader sense, permeates the education system and the news media, etc., to sell you on the idea that you are a statutory "U.S. Citizen" and "resident of the United States"(INCORPORATED).

Your Most Valuable Property is Your Signature

If you don't have calluses on your mind, then you are not thinking enough. Use your brain young king your brain! What will you do within the next 24 hours? Will you get better and stronger or bitch and complain you fucking pussy? You have been getting fucked in life because you have been a pussy. But today is the day that you learn like you never have because you're not promised tomorrow. Arise and see the opportunity. You don't have to make the same mistakes, heal get up, and get after it. Get the naysayers from around you. Your signature is your most valuable property. Your signature is your energy. You keep giving it but getting nothing back in return. That is about to change with you.

Your "property" is pledged for the rest of your life, upon your signature and your promise to perform is pledged into perpetual debt. The banksters don't even bother to go to court. They leave it up to the agencies to administer the agency's corporate public policy. It is the public policy of that agency to bill you on your promise to perform. If you don't pay, they follow up on the public policy on notice of default and give you one more chance to pay.

Then they proceed to sell the property at a tax auction. They never go to court or appear in court to back up their claim against you. Did any of your government-licensed and controlled teachers ever stress THAT YOUR SIGNATURE IS YOUR MOST VALUABLE PERSONAL PROPERTY? Did your government teachers ever tell you that any time you sign any document, you should sign it "without prejudice", or with "All Rights Reserved" above your signature?

This means you are reserving your God-given unalienable rights (rights that cannot be transferred) and all other rights for which your forefathers died. The Corporate U.S. Government provides, or at least pretends to provide, for this reservation of rights under the Uniform Commercial Code (UCC) at 1-207 and 1-103.

You need more information in this area. It is not in the best interest of the United States Corporate "Public" schools to teach you about their bankruptcy proceedings and how they have set the snare to COMPEL YOU INTO PAYING THEIR DEBT! The Corporate "Public" schools are strictly designed for their Corporate citizens/subjects.

That is, the Corporate U.S. Public School citizens. Notice all the emphasis on being a "good" citizen. All their teachers and their students are trained to produce labor and material in exchange for a valueless green paper called "money". It is not money! It functions "AS" money. Lawful money must be backed by something of value. Banksters take your labor, services, and materials (homes, cars, farms, etc.) in exchange for their valueless corporate paper. This paper is backed only by the "full faith and confidence of the United States Government" (The Mother Corporation).

The Cover-Up There was a deal struck that, if any person who doesn't have a briefcase to bring a case before the courts, and this person proves the fraud, and speaks the truth about the fraud, the courts are compelled to not allow the case to be cited or published anywhere. The courts cannot afford to have the case freely available in the public archives.
This would be evidence of the fraud. This is why you can't hire an attorney. An Attorney is compelled to uphold the fraud. "Trust Me. I am here to help you. I have the government's permission to practice law. I am a member of the BAR." The attorney is there for ONE reason.

That reason is to make sure that the bankruptcy scam (established by the corporate public policy of the corporate Federal Government) is upheld. The lawyers will cite no cases for you that will go against the bankruptcy in cooperate public policy. Whatever the lawyers do for you is a bunch of BULL ROAR. The lawyers must support the bankruptcy and public policy by supporting it, even at your expense. The lawyers can't go against the corporate Federal Government statutes of implementing, protecting, and administrating the bankruptcy.

For all cases cited, those in the U.S. Code or the state annotated code or any other source, you may be sure that they only selected those cases that support the public policy of bankruptcy. The legal system must work that way. After the last 30, 40, or 50 years of cases after cases having been decided, based upon upholding the bankruptcy, how could the legal system possibly allow someone to come into court and put in the record substantial information and argument to prove the fraud? America has been stolen. We have been made slaves: permanent debtors, bankrupt, in legal incapacity, rendered "commercial persons", "residents", and corporate franchisees knew as "citizens of the United States" under the so-called "14th Amendment". Said "Amendment" (which was never ratified - see Congressional Record, June 13, 1967; Dyett v. Turner, (1968) 439 P2d 266, 267; State v. Phillips, (1975) affirmed citizenship? The point of this is to inform Americans of their extreme plight.

We have no more country. It has been stolen - along with our lives, rights, and property. That is not paranoia, exaggeration, or hyperbole. It is a tragic truth. As a result, all "officials" are either fools or knaves, and they should no longer be complied with, or the System considered legitimate.

Suggestions and Action Steps - 1. Read and learn as much about this subject matter as you can. 2. Realize that the Government is the machinery for administering your permanent conquest, plunder, bankruptcy, and enslavement. 3. Do not pay any taxes! Every penny you pay in taxes, to your State or the Federal Government, goes to pay the phony, fraudulent "National Debt", which is unredeemable.

Every cent goes to enrich the insatiable coffers of a group of arch-charlatans, who have stolen our country and us along with it. All taxes go to finance America's plunder and subjugation. Instead of 1040's or other tax forms, send a copy of the "Public Servants" letter, with a blank tax form.

Case Law To Copy - Erie R.R. v. Thompkins, (1938) Perry v. U.S., (1935) 294 U.S. 330-381, 79 LEd 912 Dyett v. Turner, (1968) 439 P2d 266, 267 State of Utah v. Phillips, 540 P.2d 936 (1975)

An Antidote For Aphasia

4 EXPLANATIONS OF A BILL OF EXCHANGE

Too many people lose their homes because of securitization. What exactly is securitization? Securitization: The process of homogenizing financial instruments into fungible securities, so that they are sellable on the securities market.

Rules and Codes Secured Creditors Must Learn

- Article 8
- FAS125
- FAS140
- FAS5
- FAS95
- 12 USC
- GAAP and GAAS
- UCC 3-305, 306
- FAS 133
- Colorable law
- Article 9
- FR 2046
- 12 USC 248 and 347
- 12 USC 1813(L)(1)
- civil rule 13
- civil rule 36
- UCC 3-309
- HELOC
- Title 5 USC 552(b)(4)
- UCC 2-302
- Title 42 USC 4012(a)
- UCC 3-407

Example of A Bill of Exchange

If Tazadaq makes a park bench and wants to trade you for tomatoes, we can trade.

Next week if Tazadaq wants more tomatoes, but you don't want another park bench, you might accept a piece of paper that says, "Bring this to me and I will give you a park bench", and you trade or exchange that piece of paper with Qadar for a bushel of corn.
Qadar brings me "the bill" (of exchange) and I give him a picnic table.
The "Bill" was returned to the creator and the debt was extinguished. What if Qadar trades "the bill" (of exchange) to someone else? He

may figure that his picnic table will last this year, and he will get a new one next year.

That is fine, Qadar has the USE of the bill, and could even pawn the piece of paper at a pawn shop and make money by placing the piece of paper as collateral for a loan. The "bill" isn't his "property", but he is entitled to use it. The bill is still my property and remains so until the "bill" is returned to the creator and the debt is extinguished.

It is interesting to note that under this scenario, I am the surety (underwriter) of the park bench. And if people have faith that I will honor my bill, it is of useful value to others based upon the "faith and credit" of those in the exchange. i.e. Those extending credit to Qadar based upon their faith that I will perform.

It is important to know that the Pawn Shop is a creditor by "accepting my bill" and extending Qadar credit based upon their perceived value of my credit. They have the right to redeem the 'bill" with me if Qadar defaults. By connecting the dots, you can see that I have traded my labor for an interest in Qadar's enterprise if he is responsible for the pawn shop. Since it is my "bill", I could call it due and redeem the bill from the pawnshop for a park bench. Presumably, the pawn shop would agree as it is likely they gave Qadar some fraction of the generally accepted value due to this risk, and they could sell the table at a profit if Qadar defaults. But Qadar could pay the "pawn" and still get the table from them under the terms of the "pawn". The key here is that the bill is mine, and I could extinguish the "bill" if I knew where it was.

Even though the bill looks like an IOU, I am the creditor to the "creditor" (pawn shop) because it is my creditworthiness that allowed the Pawn Shop to extend credit to Qadar. It was not entirely Qadar's creditworthiness.

The Pawnshop is in the same position that the Federal Reserve takes when they accept your signature on the Private side and issue Public funds to banks. They change the venue from private to public. The Federal Reserve has agreed to accept the signatures of private people for whatever they want if the people go through their licensed intermediaries (banks).

An Antidote For Aphasia

The banks have agreed to withhold access to the private venue for incompetents by their license agreements. If you are incompetent, (not creditworthy) they will decide how much they will loan you in public.

The banks must report all transactions on this change of venue to the Federal Reserve as the Federal Reserve knows that you should "redeem" your credit and they will give it to you when you are deemed competent. They have an awesome accounting program that they have developed internally, called not surprisingly, the Internal RE–VENUE Service.

An understanding of fractals is helpful at this point, but essentially nature performs the same functions over and over in repeating patterns.

The monetary system is based on this concept.

Everything is returned to the creator.

You were created by something, and you will be returned to the creator when you are 'extinguished'.

During the time that you are here, you get to "borrow" everything that has been created, but since you didn't create it, you don't "OWN" it. You just get the use of it. – usufruct –

It is like trust. The creator is the grantor, and you are the trustee (entrusted with the use of the planet) and are responsible for the care of it. Children are the beneficiaries of this trust. Once they become competent, they become trustees as well.

If they do not become competent and do not manage their affairs consistent with the care of the planet, the fractal nature of nature is that they will create conditions that accelerate their demise, much like yeast cells that overproduce alcohol and cause the yeast culture to die. The money system is the same way, it will fail if there are no responsible people – as we have today….and the warning signs are very clear.

The government has adopted a similar strategy for the monetary system, based upon the exchange of energy inputs.

Your energy is exchanged for something of value.

An Antidote For Aphasia

You have the unlimited right to contract and only you can place a value on your labor, and the price you will pay for a car.
Now let's examine the essence of the currency system by recalling the picnic table scenario.

If I am the government and I want to increase the ease of commercial transactions (trade) I may offer to create uniform bills of exchange if the people agree to it. The value proposition to me is that I will charge a fee for my energy in creating and managing the "units", and my people will benefit from not having to lug around heavy gold, silver, or picnic tables to conduct trade.

It speeds interaction for "picnic table builders" as they do not have to search to find a trader for picnic tables, they pledge their labor in return for a stable currency that allows them to quickly obtain what they need by "passing the buck" as a representation that they are a productive member of society since they have obtained "units" somehow.

Monetary policy is based upon scarcity. If sand were money, you would need to bring a dump truck to trade for a kernel of corn.
Nature is based upon abundance. How much do you pay for the sunlight and water that grows your corn? It is free from the creator. You trade your labor for the care of weeding the field and you can sell the free corn because you labored to ensure (responsible trustee) the crop comes in.

There is a balance between the two, monetary policy is based upon productive (responsible trustees) to create value.
Monetary policy=scarcity - it is a construct or an idea. Fiction
Nature=Abundance. – it is tangible. Non-Fiction.
If you operate in nature and trade your crops for chairs and things you need, you don't need "units of credit"
If you operate using the fictional idea of money, then you must obey the fictional rules of money just as you must obey the rules of nature to grow your corn.

Let's say that I (the government) am appointed to manage the money system (or I appoint someone to do it for me.) The first thing that we would have to do is decide how many units to create. Do we create as many units as there are grains of sand? Or do we create one unit per person? – Assuming that everyone is equal (the presumption of the Constitution) We may start by creating 13 units for the 13 people I have in my government.

The people have created the "authority" for me to do this, so technically it is their "will" and their property if they ask for it. They can trade these units among themselves. At the end of the year, just like the game Monopoly, there will be a temporary uneven distribution of the units to those people who have learned how to cater to the needs of others.

This distribution is based upon the "vote" of the people. If they value Tulip Bulbs, then the Tulip Growers will end up with a disproportionate amount of the units. If people value Elvis Presley's songs, Elvis gets his due. The system doesn't care who you vote for. You have the unlimited right to contract for services. Everybody gets what they want, and everything is in balance.

Since I don't know how productive each member will be I will issue additional credits to each member of my "society" upon their pledge (signature) if they will go through an intermediary (bank) who I will delegate the responsibility of blocking credit access to this private side of the ledger for incompetents. I can't have the "children" getting whatever they want if they are not responsible/competent. Once they claim their exemption-which requires a fair amount of competency- they are deemed to be competent and will be deemed to have reached the age of majority and can join the free society and be a trustee/beneficiary to the commonwealth of the society. Or the Commonwealth.

What happens when my 13 people become 26 people (due to childbirth? Hmmm…I need to create more units so each of the children has their own unit too. I will need to track the birth levels in each county, and I recognize that the children will probably not be "productive" until they are 18, so I may just create 18 units per child as soon as they are born. I assume that the child will be grateful that I "the creator" of the money advanced them these units and they will return via their labor via a pledge from their mother to me.

Since the child is not going to use all 18 units right up front, I may place the units in trust for the child and allow the child to claim them when they need them, but in the meantime, I will invest the unclaimed units in highly productive assets for the good of my nation.

If they are exceptionally productive children, like Bill Gates, I may find that they have produced for the nation/government far more than the original 18 units and they are entitled to the additional PRIVATE units created, if they ask for them. I will withhold this credit for incompetents. —See withholding IRS regs.

I presume that they will ask for them when they reach the age of majority and are competent to make decisions. If I don't hear from them by the time they are 18, they are presumed incompetent, and I will withhold their access to their private credit as they are not responsible, or I may presume they must have died.

I will begin to probate the assets that are in their account for the good of the public rather than waste the units as they have been brought from the private into the public and the investment is needed to offset interest is being paid since I cannot count on any productive labor from a dead or incompetent body. I will place the extra units in CAFR funds.

They are incompetent because they are creating more debt by not discharging/extinguishing their bills. I have chartered the banks to return abandoned units to me and I will extinguish the debt myself after giving 36 months to the creator to extinguish the debt on their own. I will continue to withhold access to private credit to incompetents.

Incompetents in the public further demonstrate incompetence in a fractal way by financing their demise, (nature has a way of doing this).

Consider your actions at the store when you must choose between $2.00 factory-raised eggs and the $4.00 free-range eggs. If you live in scarcity, you may choose the eggs based on price, not nutrients. In your retirement fund, you invest in Halliburton because you want a 20% return on your "money".

You get the kind of government you deserve because you VOTE for it every day with a representation of your energy. In the theatre of the mind, it is not survival of the fittest, it is survival of the reflective. The world reflects our collective choices, and if you are not "reflecting" on your decisions, you are controlled by the other side of the mirror, the reflection of your shadow. So, what kind of world are you creating? Are you controlling it or letting it control you? In the system what exactly DO you create? Analogous to the picnic table scenario, you may not create picnic tables, but you are ultimately the creditor. Banks cannot loan their assets by law. So, what exactly do you create?

MONEY
When you go to a bank you are an authorized representative of the bank to create money.
Your signature creates the money that allows the public to exchange units.
If you created the money with your signature, it is just like creating a picnic table.

That is an exceptionally simplistic overview of the nature of fiat currency creation, but the important thing to understand is that currency is a fractal (fictional) version of nature …like electricity. It flows like currents in a river and flow is corrected by banks. If you resist the fictional rules of fictional money, you are a "resistor" and you will be "charged" and brought before a "circuit" court (the bank will correct you) and if you do not "discharge" (counterclaim) the matter, you will be placed in a "cell" until the energy is returned to the source/creator (you), otherwise you are "grounded".
If you don't understand public and private, look at a dollar bill and see that you have been given notice that there are two sides to a dollar "bill" and it is good for all debts public and private.

So, let's look at the second level of currency creation.
Securitization. It is called that because it is based on your social security account which has two sides to it. A public and a private side. The SSN is public, and the red numbers on the back are private. Incompetents operate in the public, and "components" operate in the private. It is your bill, and it must be returned to you.

Kahan Tazadaq Shah

An Antidote For Aphasia

KAHAN TAZADAQ A SPOKES MAN4 MEN

RED PILL
RIGHT KNOWLEDGE
"REGENERATED"

Order now @ www.kahantazadaq.net

5 AFTER YOU SIGN A MORTGAGE NOTE IF FALLS UNDER UCC ARTICLE 3: RECOUPMENT

It is a cash payment. It IS the money for the house.
A "security" is an interest in future payments.
A financial instrument that represents: an ownership position in a publicly- traded corporation (stock), a creditor relationship with a governmental body or a corporation (bond), or rights to ownership as represented by an option. A security is a fungible, negotiable financial instrument that represents some type of financial value. The company or entity that issues the security is known as the issuer.

Definition of 'Securitization'
The process through which an issuer creates a financial instrument by combining other financial assets and then marketing different tiers of the repackaged instruments to investors. The process can encompass any type of financial asset and promotes liquidity in the marketplace.

After securitization, it comes under Article 8. Under US law securitization is illegal because it is fraudulent. Instruments such as loans, credit cards, and receivables, are securitized. Enron was involved in securitization, and someone brought charges against them. But almost all large corporations are doing it as usual business. However, the banking system and the government are also doing it.

It is all accounting, whether it is banking, civil or criminal court. Submit the FASB regulations – FAS125 securitization accounting, FAS140 Offsetting of financial assets and liabilities, FAS 133 derivatives on hedge accounts, FAS5, FAS95. These are the resource materials for understanding this process.

The note is not under a negotiable instrument anymore, it is a security. All the banks follow these standards. They set up GAAP, generally accepted accounting principles. The banks are mandated by Title 12 USC to follow GAAP and GAAS. They have a local FASB and an international IFASB. They also cover derivatives. FAS 140 relates to UCC 3-305, 306. If you want to instruct them on how to do offsets, you must refer them to FAS 133. If you don't know the accounting regulations, you can't give them the proper instructions for settling and closing.

The goal is Recoupment
Recoupment – (1) The recovery or regaining of expenses Applying the setoff so you can get back what you gave and what you are entitled to.
(2) The withholding for the equitable part or all of something due. This is all equitable action in admiralty-style instruments.
Blacks:
IOU – a memorandum acknowledging a debt. See also a due bill.
DUE BILL – See IOU
SIGHT DRAFT – A draft that is due on the bearer's demand, or on proper presentment to the drawer. Also termed a demand draft. A draft is an unconditional order signed by one person, the drawer directing another person, the drawee, to pay a certain sum of money on demand or at a definite time to a person, the payee, or to bearer.

It's colorable

Who is holding the debt? A due bill is like a sight draft. They are not saying from which perspective it is a debt, from theirs or yours. The party receiving the IOU is the debtor because the IOU is an asset. It is an instrument, and you are the originator. You have monetized their system with your signature. An IOU is an asset instrument, not a liability instrument. This is one of the places where you have your perspective changed.

Who is holding the debt? A due bill is like a sight draft. They are not saying from which perspective it is a debt, from theirs or yours. The party receiving the IOU is the debtor because the IOU is an asset. It is an instrument, and you are the originator. You have monetized their system with your signature. An IOU is an asset instrument, not a liability instrument. This is one of the places where you have your perspective changed.

We the people have the Power

An Antidote For Aphasia

Under the constitution, the government was not given authority to create money. It is a power reserved by the people. Article I, section 10 restricted the states from making gold coins. So, the corporate government must rely on the ignorance of people to create money. So the way money is created is to have people sign an IOU or promissory note... It is not a debt instrument to the one who created it; it is an asset. The creator can pass it on for someone else to use. It is negotiable unless it includes terms and conditions as part of a contract. The property belongs to the creator, and the holder is merely using it and any proceeds that come from it should be restored to the creator.

That is the power we have if we realize we have the authority to do this. The intent is to understand the regulations and to see how they accept our ignorance to believe we are the debtor and the slave, and they are always the creditor. This is not true if you are competent. We are looking for recoupment.

Once we, the creator of the promissory note, have signed it and others are using it, recoupment means we want our property back or have the account set off. Recoupment in practice is a counterclaim in a civil procedure. That is how one does a recoupment. We did a counterclaim because; with the county, you can do a setoff. You can use the financial liability of the accounting ledger to offset the financial asset if you have the right to do that. But you have the right to do that if you are the creditor on the liability side and the bank or lending institution is the debtor on the liability side.

There is a duality here. The bank is the creditor on the receivable side or their asset side that is the receivable. You are the creditor on the liability side of the accounts payable. You can use your accounts payable as an offset or counterclaim to the financial asset side that is the receivable. The bank or the court is using the receivable side of the accounting ledger. That is what they are charging you with. On the receivable side, you must pay the debt, because that is where the charge is coming from since they are claiming to be the creditor like a bank collecting the mortgage.

An Antidote For Aphasia

6 THEY ARE DOUBLE ENTRY BOOKKEEPING

The mortgage side of the bank ledger is the bank's assets and their receivables. But on the liability side, because they sold our gold... (1933 EO- Franklin Roosevelt)
We have the actual gold contract where they did this. This is not my opinion; we have eleven $50 million gold bonds sold from the DeBeers Diamond Company. They sold America's gold under contract to the Bank of China. This is not my opinion. The U.S. did not go bankrupt in 1933.

What they did was sell all the gold under a gold contract to the Chinese government. So, the U.S. had to give us an account payable as a cash receipt. FAS 95 tells us that when they do credit to a transactional account, which is a liability account, on which we are the creditor, they give a cash receipt to the customer and a cash payment to the bank, because it is cash proceeds. In intermediate accounting, when you give them a promissory note.

Your Negotiable Instruments Always Works.

Kahan Tazadaq gave a promissory note to a publisher for $1900. They accepted it because I gave them the proper accounting instructions. I did another one to another publisher for over $5000. They accepted initially and then hired a collection attorney in one of the biggest collection agencies in the state of Ohio. They didn't send the note back because a payment tendered and refused was discharged. Also, any form of viable payment must be accepted. Almost anyone that you send a note to is going to be making a mistake if they send it back.

There is someone here who sent a transaction to the IRS on a closed checking account. He got the canceled check back from the IRS. They said the check was no good because it was a closed account. But the transactional marks on the back of the check say otherwise.

If it is a note put into a bank, it is a cash receipt to the depositor and a cash payment to the Bank. So, when the bank processed that closed

check, the IRS got a cash receipt and the bank got cash payment. Then the IRS sent it back, so it is evidence that the transaction was accepted, but then colorable and publicly claimed it was no good.
The publisher accepted the note and hired an attorney. I sent them a letter and they dropped the matter since they know that I know what accounting is. Under FAS 140, you get your setoff. When you make a deposit, it is a cash receipt, a cash proceeds. Everything becomes cash proceeds in commercial law under Article 9. They show it as a cash proceed. They give you a credit to your account that is a cash receipt to you the customer or the borrower. Then they make a cash payment to the bank. The bank sells notes. They do a HELOC, home equity line of credit, and sell it to a warehouse lending institution. This is the same as a credit card. Even on a mortgage loan.

A HELOC is different than warehouse lending. I got this from their mortgage department. They take the proceeds from the promissory note and pay off the warehouse lender. So, the debt on the real estate is extinguished from the books (that is why they call it closing).

They are required to file FR 2046. This is a balance sheet. Under 12 USC 248 and 347, they are required to file a balance sheet. They are required on a quarterly or weekly basis. They file these balance sheets with the Federal Reserve Board. I talked to the head of the FRB. They file a balance sheet with the board. The balance sheet shows the assets and liabilities that they use in the accounting. The liabilities would be your promissory note. It is a liability because it is an asset to you.

Securitization is the process of transferring all the liabilities off the balance sheet. They can do this because you never ask for them. They have everybody conned into believing we are debtors instead of creditors and do not know how to ask for our assets. We never ask for recoupment. So why carry the payables in the books if they have been abandoned? Why not write them off and sell them for more cash?

The government has such complicated books it is impossible to

figure out what is going on.
If you give a bank a promissory note, they are required to give you a cash receipt. They owe you that money under a recoupment or asset. If you take the receipt back, they should give you some money. They call it an offset in accounting, but in the UCC it is called a recoupment. Unless you do ask or do a defense in recoupment under UCC 3-305, and a claim under 3-306, you have a possessory and property claim against the cash proceeds under the liability side of the ledger. UCC 3-306, there cannot be a holder in due course on a promissory note after they deposit it. They do an off-balance sheet entry.

This means they take your note after they sell it, instead of showing it on their balance sheet, they move over to some other entity's balance sheet. It is no longer in the bank's books.

The Balance Sheets Were Moved

This is called off-balance sheet bookkeeping. The head of the FASB said that I was correct. They are not showing the liability side of the ledger or the accounts payable because it has been moved over to someone else's balance sheet.
The IRS does the same thing when you tender them a negotiable instrument. They accept it and never return it. But don't adjust the account. They pretend like nothing happened. They move them off the books that the collection agent is looking at. He is only looking at the accounts receivable ledger.

You tender a note to the bank to stop foreclosure, and they ignore it. The agent at the bank claims she never got any payment. The agent only sees the receivable side of the books. He is being honest. It is up to us to make a claim for them to look at their other set of books. You must learn how the system works so you can explain it to them. We need to know how to get them to produce the missing documents. They are only going to produce the documents that support their claim. The American and English litigation system is adversarial. They only must present the evidence that supports their claim. So, do you

Creditor Moves
When a strawman is charged with speeding, he is given a charging instrument. It is the same as a claim by the bank that shows that someone has failed to make a mortgage payment. It is a commercial entry from a corporation showing that there is a liability on your part that is an account receivable, and they are in the capacity of a creditor and making you appear in the capacity of a debtor. So the clerk has an accounting charge against the strawman but you are operating the account. It is your responsibility to bring in recoupment on behalf of the real party of interest which is you because you are the ultimate creditor if you raise that claim against the liability side of the account.

People have a right to travel. So, they have the right of recoupment to offset any charges against the strawman in an attempt to restrict the right of travel of living people. Civil and criminal court procedures operate the same as the bank.

Ignore-ANCE – Ignoring the facts before your eyes.
What is the substantive principle involved in this that allows them to avoid fraud? The government does everything correctly. They never make a mistake. The government is involved in securitization which appears to be fraudulent. There is immunity for people who understand the procedure. Only the unlearned are fooled into voluntarily entering fraudulent contracts. It does not work if you get frustrated and angry at the fraudulent results of your ignorance.

Your Promissory Note Created the Money

When you sign a promissory note to create the mortgage with a bank to buy your house, at closing, they have already sold your note to the warehousing institution. The warehousing institution brought money into the bank when they bought the note. At closing, they take the money and close out the account on one side. The bank forgot to tell you that you don't have a liability on their receivable side anymore.

Why do they keep taking your money? They have become the servicer for the account; they are not paying principal and interest. The payments are profit to the holder of the note. This is not stealing if we know how to claim recoupment. They are using the notes to expand the money supply.

Under Title 12 USC 1813(L)(1) when you deposit a promissory note, it becomes a cash item. It becomes the equivalent of cash because I have a cash receipt. I talked to Walker Todd, one of the heads of the Cleveland FRB. He has been a government witness in court cases regarding BOE. He said that I was correct that we are the creditors on the payables side of the ledger. The bank owes you the money. No one is bringing up recoupment as a defense. You waive the defense, and they go to collection on the receivables.

Under civil rule 13, you fail to bring a mandatory counterclaim, which is based on the same transaction. Under the rules you have waived it because you were ignorant of the rules of the procedure.
Kahan Tazadaq filed a motion in a court case. He took portions of Statement 95 and incorporated it into a memorandum. These reports are filed on OMB forms in which the public has a right to disclosure under the privacy act.

If they shift the assets off the books, they must report to the FRB where it went, so you can follow it. In the memorandum, it shows that they are mandated to give a cash receipt on any deposit. It is a demand deposit account. They are required to show it in their books, but they are not doing that. They are doing an offset entry. This is not going to trial because we are going to subpoena the auditor. Auditors keep track of where the assets went. These are special auditors.

We have asked for all this information in discovery under civil rule 36if they don't answer, they have admitted them. This is so powerful in this foreclosure that the bank's attorney is saying that discovery and records from auditors do not constitute admissions. Ha! Are you telling the court that the bank's records kept in the due course of business are not admissions? They are hurting.

So, in our motion for summary judgment, I put in admissions that they admitted by non-response. So now we have them in a dilemma.

The other side is scrambling. They have come out with an affidavit for a lost note or destroyed instrument.

Under UCC 3-309 you must show four elements to claim a lost instrument:
1) you were in possession at the time it was lost.
2) you have the right to enforce of the note.
3) you have to show that the obligor on the note is indemnified by you against any future claims.
4) the loss was not due to a transfer.

They are trying to maintain the illusion that they are still holding your paperwork because you are still paying them. The illusion is that there is a debt that is due.

I've got the S3 registration statement. That is the form the bank filed that they sold the note which is a transfer. The attorney lied when he put in a claim that the instrument was lost.

We have the 424(b)(5) prospectus. The bank we are dealing with is Bank One which is owned by JP Morgan and Chase. They sold it in 1997 right after they got our loan they sold it. They are doing a HELOC. Most banks do warehouse lending. As soon as they get the note, they borrow the money from a warehouse lender. The bank does not give you money or credit. They get it from a warehouse lender. Then they pay off the warehouse lender with the note that they sell to them. Then they make derivatives out of this note by a bookkeeping entry.

The balance sheet, a 2046, 2049, and 2099, have OMB numbers on them that are subject to disclosure under the privacy act, Title 5 USC **552(b)(4).**

They must give it to you if you ask for it. At closing and settlement, the reason they call it closing is because they pay off the loan in its entirety. The debt is extinguished.

The patriots say they didn't lend any money. But that doesn't rebut the receivable. There is no money. But we loaned them the note. So we started the process, so we have to help resolve the problem.

They do the accounting appropriately, but there are two sets of books. But if you don't ask to see the books, it is your problem. This is also what they are doing in the courtroom. The clerk has the receivable side for the corporation and the judge has the payables.

The judge is holding accounts payable under HJR 192 for all the people who come before him if he has the SSN. The judge is not required to be a witness or bring pleadings to court. He is a referee. The receivables are the charges against the strawman. The party aware of the payables is not the same party handling the receivables. People don't bring in an offsetting claim under the rules of procedure.

The judge does not have to do the setoff unless you raise the issue or defense. We have the right to waive it. So, the judge is the priest receiving the sacrifice for the corporation.

An Antidote For Aphasia

Scan QR Code

Open the page on your phone by scanning the QR Code with the camera.

An Antidote For Aphasia

An Antidote For Aphasia

creditor moves kahan tazadaq the GOAT

7 SECURITIZATION II

Levy on Paycheck
Employer filed Form 1096 to pay Corp income tax with employee's salary and using accounts payable Direct Treasury Account.
Use Form 1099-OID, corrected box checked Form 1096 and 1040, for a refund. Kahan Tazadaq's letter to Bill Collector law firm:

Dear Mr. John Doe,
I, Kahan Tazadaq, am writing regarding your recent letter regarding your client ABC CORP, being the alleged creditor for $1700. Your alleged client waived their status as a creditor when they accepted my tender of payment under UCC §§3-409(a)&(b) and UCC §3-604(a). They did not adjust their accounting ledger to reflect the settlement and closure of the accounts receivable side of the accounting ledger.
By way of review, I sent the woman in the credit department of the creditor, a negotiable instrument on April 24th in the form of a commercial note draft, as an order to pay under UCC 3- 104(e). This may be treated either as a promise to pay or an order to pay. Since she has not returned the instrument to me, she has chosen the latter; an order to pay.

Under §3-104(f) of the UCC a draft is the equivalent of a check and may be securitized or monetized by direct deposit in a commercial checking, time, thrift, or savings account under **Title 12 of the United States Code, Section 1813(L)(1)** and when deposited it becomes the equivalent of money as outlined under **Section 1813(L)(1).**

The collection manager from the credit department of the creditor did, however, send me a letter saying that she did not accept promissory notes. She is, however, precluded by public policy HJR-192 and Title 31 of the United States Code Section 5118(d)(2), and the Fair Debt Practices Act, aka, Consumer Protection Act at 15 USC §1601 and §1693 from demanding payment in any specific coin or currency of the United States, even though she has not done so.
Section (d)(2) of Title 31 USC
§1518 states that an obligation governed by gold coin is discharged

on payment dollar for dollar, by United States coin or currency that is a legal tender at the time of payment. The narrow view that money is limited to legal tender is rejected under **Section 1-201(24) of the UCC.** It is not limited to United States dollars. See official comments under section 3-104 of the UCC under the definition of money.

The man at the creditor has failed to perform his duty as fiduciary trustee of the account. I have done a Notarial protest against him and the account for non-acceptance and payment under **sections 3-501 and 3-505(a)(b) of the UCC,** which creates the evidence or presumption of dishonor.

He knowingly or unknowingly becomes the debtor and me the creditor by operation of commercial and administrative law. Also worthy of note, if she is going to treat the note as a liability instrument, she must present it to me for payment and make me chargeable under 3-501 of the UCC, which she has also failed to do. To the extent that she is in dishonor for non-acceptance and nonpayment by Notarial protest on the administrative side, ... there has been a discharge of the debt in its entirety under the Fair Debt Collection Practices Act within the 30-day time frame as mandated by law.

I have been teaching and studying commercial banking law and intermediate and advanced accounting for 36 years. I have a degree in Commercial Banking law, four years of undergraduate study at USC, and four years at Hastings School of Law in San Francisco. This is for your edification and exhortation.

Since I am reasonably sure that we can come to a peaceful resolution of this matter, as your client does not understand commercial banking law, and the **IASB, the FASB, and GAAP** principles as they apply to commercial banking. I do a lot of trading and purchasing in commodities and securities exchange markets where the use of revocable standby letters of credit, documentary drafts, international bills of exchange, or promissory notes are used exclusively under the UNICITRAL convention.

An Antidote For Aphasia

Your client is not applying the correct accounting entries under GAAP. She is treating the account as a trade receivable through securitization as an off-balance sheet financing technique. Since she has accepted the instrument that I have tendered, I have a claim or possessory right in the instrument and its proceeds under 3-306 of the UCC. Any defense and any claim in recoupment under section 3-305 of the UCC, which I shall exercise at my option if she does not credit my account.

The 1099-OID will identify who the principal is from, which capital and interest were taken, who the recipient or who the payer of the funds is, and who is holding the account in escrow and unadjusted. Since I am solution-oriented and want to show good faith, there are two ways of resolving this matter.

Since your client has already accepted my tender of payment and has not returned it, you can instruct her to credit my account for the sum said in full for settlement and closure. Or instruct her to return the original instrument to me, unendorsed, and I will make an alternative form of payment. Otherwise, I will consider this matter settled and closed.
END OF LETTER

The man at the creditor can't send the promissory note back because he has already negotiated the instrument. No one ever gets promissory notes or BOEs returned because a debt tendered and refused is discharged. He kept the note and wrote a letter saying that she doesn't accept promissory notes. But his actions speak louder than words. She accepted it. So, it has already gone into the corporate liability account, but it didn't go into the corporate asset account for the ledger. A debt tendered and refused is a debt paid.

Kahan Tazadaq sent an IBOE to a bank and they negotiated it and said they returned it. But they didn't return it. They deposited it and it became cash proceeds. So, whenever you send them the note or BOE, they keep it in their deposit system, and it becomes a cash item. They get a cash receipt for the deposit. If you don't understand accounting, they get away with the theft of your instrument. You gave them the instrument to settle and close the account. Your instrument is an asset to you. It appears that you created a debt instrument, but the opposite is true. The government has no authority under the constitution to create money. So only the people can create money.

So, we are the originators of money, so we are the creditors. But they make you believe you are the debtor as if they are the creator of money.
The only way you have an accounting of the instrument is in the bookkeeping. And they are keeping the account on the off-balance sheet ledger. If they know you know what they are doing, they won't try to hide it.

When they go to a collection agency, they are selling the account as a trade receivable from the asset side of the bank's ledger. If the bank is trying to collect money, the evidence that debt owed on their books is on their asset ledger, accounts receivable. If you gave them a promissory note, they must record a debt to you on their liability ledger. When the US citizens became enemies of the state in 1933, they were not required to notify them of their assets. They are not required to notify enemies of their assets during times of war. They are not required to return enemies of their assets. So, they are kept in hidden books.

When you send the collection agency the above letter it creates a fiduciary duty for them to go back to the principal to check the off-balance sheet liability ledger to determine if the account has been paid and if your claim is correct. This principle applies to the IRS and the courts. They only want to discuss what you owe them and ignore what you pay them. The reason they tell you that your negotiable instrument is no good is that under the Trading With the Enemy Act, they cannot allow you to create your negotiable instruments or use your assets. All they have done is keep the ledgers separate. The receivables book has not been pledged. That is why the collection agent says they have not given you credit, and you still owe the money.

The debt collector buys the account receivable in good faith without evidence of its accuracy. It is like a charging instrument. The attorney says pay up or we are coming after you. Under civil rules of procedure, rule 13, commerce is adversarial, so they are not required to tell you the whole truth. It is mandated that the defendant returns a counterclaim with facts proving that the charge is untrue, which is an affirmative defense. A claim is an account that has matured for debt collection. You must show you are a creditor. The charge is a presumptive claim with no evidence.

A notice of lien or levy has no evidence of a claim.

It is just a charge. A notice is a claim of jurisdiction. A counterclaim is not a dispute or argument. Disputes are not permitted. If the merchant had brought a claim, it would have been a fraud, because you already paid it. So, they just give you a presumptive notice. It is an unsupported charge. There is a probable cause with no evidence. You must respond to it because it will become valid if you don't. It is just a notice of interest.

It can mature into a claim with your failure to respond. You must accept it and return it with your notice of interest, which is a counterclaim, within 10 days, according to admiralty rules. Failure to do a specific negative averment of the facts alleged (rule 9) constitutes an acceptance of this fact as far as the courts are concerned. A notice of interest matures to the agreement of the parties that they have a valid claim, so they do not have to prove it.

You Must object
An unsupported notice of interest becomes an agreed claim. They are not guilty of fraud, deceit, or trickery. Your failure to respond is the problem. Our responsibility is to rebut the assumptions and presumptions under the rules of evidence.

Jean did everything he needed to do in-laws and at-law to resolve the issue. The merchant handling the books was only handling the accounts receivable books for the corporation and was not privy to their accounts payable books, which are their liability books. The reason the corporations separate their bookkeeping is they can bring this woman in with a straight face and no knowledge that the other books exist, swear in court that she's been handling these books for years and the account still has a $1500 balance. You sent in an instrument that had nothing to do with affecting the balance on the books she handles. When that corporation did a deposit of your promissory note, or BOE as a cash item receipt, that went into the other set of books that she doesn't see. She can use her affidavit and swear that this account is still open. Whereas if you knew the accountant on the other set of books, and subpoenaed those books, you would find something on the ledger over there and there hasn't been a transfer or exchange of information between the two sets of books.

You need to bring the knowledge of that forward to a data integrity board hearing. "I don't disagree with anything that this lady is saying, however, if you would go over to the corporate liability off-balance sheet ledgers, you would find that there has been a set off deposited there and if you could see both sets of books, you would see there is a set-off, which is a claim under civil rule 13, which I am timely invoking and I am asking you to look at both sets of books and do the offset balance and do the settlement and closure in this matter.

Remember, the firm hired an attorney collection firm. The collector came with the charge to Tazadaq. How many times has Tazadaq been charged by different entities in this case? Twice, so they can have two or more witnesses. The first time he said to the receivable lady with the merchant, here is a promissory note. She determined that she was not going to accept it. But the note didn't come back. So now the corporation sells the account to an attorney and the attorney writes a letter to Tazadaq. Tazadaq raised a rule 13 affirmative defense in his letter back. Showing by the accounting what the problem was and describing the claim he would make in court.

This attorney's company is the second set of witnesses acting as the data integrity board trying to find out why you haven't paid. So, you should give them your records so they can compare your records with the corporation's records and decide whose records are correct.

An Antidote For Aphasia

Let him know that ONE, you did not get the note back, so they are a holder, so they are liable for it. TWO, this was meant as a set off on the corporate liability books because they kept my note. They should have given him a cash receipt for the note. The woman in receivables is only looking at the corporate asset ledger. That is an affirmative defense and a set-off claim that the law can recognize.

Matthew 5:25 Agree with thine adversary quickly whiles thou art in the way with him; lest at any time the adversary deliver thee to the judge, and the judge deliver thee to the officer, and thou be cast into prison.

The attorney's company can either go back to the corporation and close the case or else if it goes to court, this is going to be my affirmative defense and my counterclaim in court because I have an asset that the corporation is holding of mine, that they failed to give me credit for. Where they made the mistake that they are likely carrying my assets on a liability ledger of balance from their accounts receivable. What I am asking you to do, as a data integrity board, is to investigate to determine which one of us has the most sustainable evidence.

The attorney firm was put there as an opportunity for you to have a second witness to investigate the matter and settle the account. They don't usually have to investigate the information that is sold to them by the corporation. They don't have any probable cause to believe differently. In an adversarial system, it is up to you to tell your side of the story. Every debt collector writes in his letter; "If you have any reason to dispute this debt, let us know." You have to send them your claim within 10 or 30 days. Do not argue or create a dispute. Simply give them the facts of your defense.

Kahan Tazadaq put in his note: A promise to pay, an order to pay, and a notice of tender of payment and asked them to credit it to the accounts receivable. He should also have asked for a cash receipt. It would be fraud if the corporation kept after Jean, so they sold the receivable to a third party that doesn't know the whole story.

An Antidote For Aphasia

They are a new party. When a new party comes after you, they have no standing under the UCC to do it. But if you argue, it causes a new controversy. All you do is present your claim that shows you are the creditor in the transaction. The new holder has to be the data integrity board. So, he is your best opportunity to settle and close. Don't ignore him.

The IRS has a notice of lien or levy. It is a charge or notice of interest. Don't argue with them. You should rebut it under civil rule 13. Otherwise, it stands as fact, and they don't have to prove anything. The government and their agents are here to test us. If we want to pass the test, we should have a claim for set off. We must act like creditors, not debtors. Yahusha paid for all our debts.

Kahan Tazadaq did the Notarial protest on the note. It becomes the evidence that you put in your claim. You must register the note on a UCC3, to make it a public record. Lisa used a note to discharge her parole. However, she did not register the note on her UCC3. So, it was never recognized by the public to settle and close the matter. So, her charge was sold to a Hong Kong company that requires a wanted notice maintained on her as their notice of interest.

You don't need any evidence to issue a notice of interest. IRS notices of lien or levy are just notices of interest. You have 10 to 30 days to respond with a counterclaim. If you don't respond, they have a claim by default. Arguing creates the IRS claim by default. We are a creditor when we discharge the debt, but we never respond timely with a counterclaim to show we are a creditor. Since the IRS is just a debt collector, they are the best place to have a data integrity board hearing to settle and close the matter.

Arguments about the law are not counterclaims. If we don't bring a claim, we lose. If we discharge the debt, and they keep the note, we have a claim as a creditor. The note cannot be introduced as evidence of the claim. If they kept the note without giving a receipt, your record is the UCC registration of the note. Don't put the invoice AR4V on the UCC. It is a liability, not an asset. The BOE becomes a registered security under UCC article 8, which is superior to other UCC articles. The court will not look at any security that is not registered in the public.

You should register your bank mortgage note on your UCC 3, to establish a claim. The mortgage note is a security, and it is never registered. The finance system is dealing in unregistered securities. They cannot take an unregistered mortgage note into court for foreclosure. They never produce a note of foreclosure because it is evidence of their liability and not cognizable in court. We are the creditors on the mortgage note, so we should register it. As soon as we register the mortgage note, we become the creditor in the foreclosure case with the highest interest.

If we tendered a BOE to settle and close a criminal case, it should be registered. The clerk never gave us an accounting for credit. **So, they will ignore it because we didn't make the rule 13 counterclaim.** We must register the BOE on a UCC3 and bring a UCC11 in as a counterclaim. All other arguments do not matter because all law is an illusion. They converted everything to a commercial transaction at the beginning of the case.

People have filed UCC liens listing the bank as the debtor. The debtor should be the prepaid account at the Secretary of Treasury of Puerto Rico. The strawman should be a third-party creditor because he is a bailee on another filing. The living man does not appear in their system, so the strawman must be the creditor. All parties on a UCC filing must be fiction, not living. The SSN is the account number. The living man is responsible for all transactions.

THE ANTIDOTE FOR APHASIA

THE WAR AGAINST COGNITIVE DISSONANCE

BY KAHAN TAZADAQ

GHTEOUS WOMEN ARE GO
KAHAN TAZADAQ SHAH

8 RULE 11

When Kahan Tazadaq sent his claim to the collection agency, they had the fiduciary responsibility to go back to the corporation and ask to see the off-balance-sheet liabilities ledger to check out the claim. When you give them notice, they must go to discovery under civil rule 11.

He must find out who is responsible for the accounts payable ledger and what did with the cash receipt for his deposit. I want to see your 1099-OID, statement 95 cash flow statement, and your balance sheet. Kahan will not likely hear from these people again. Jean presented a credible counterclaim. The note was an asset to him and a liability to the corporation and they didn't account for it.

The debt collector can't resell the receivable now, because he has had notice. The sale would not have been in good faith. The woman in the original company was operating in ignorant good faith. She only saw half the books. You may have to go through the administrative procedure against him if he ignores your claim. After he has seen both sides of the book, he would be operating in fraud. The Enron executives that got in trouble were the ones who saw both sides of the book. Securitization is fraud.
Some companies pass the receivable on to fourth or fifth parties so they can have clean hands. But no one ever told them about the second set of books.

We have not given them registered security.
There is no evidence in the public record.
They can carry the illusion that your instrument is worthless, forever.
If we do not understand that the collection agent only sees the receivables and not the payables, we will fail to state a claim.
This puts us into commercial dishonor, which gives them the option to take us to court to force us to pay in Federal Reserve notes.
So, the first court case is an appeal from the administrative process.
One is not allowed to introduce a new claim in an appeal.
The factual hearing was with the collection agency. We are foreclosed

from bringing our claim. One must raise the claim at the appropriate time, or you have not exhausted your administrative remedies. We need to get a data integrity review hearing or a secondary hearing because we have new evidence to be adjudicated.

The Truth-in-lending Act (TILA), section 226.23, which is regulation Z, gives one the right to rescind any commercial debt contract or agreement entered.

All commercial contracts for credit or loan provide 72 hours to do a rescission. That can be extended for three years from the date that one discovers that one did not have full disclosure. In Appendix H, it says that this regulation Z does not apply to residential mortgage transactions. However, once foreclosure has been initiated on a mortgage, one can rescind it if; (a) they did not disclose the right to rescind at closing under Appendix H. They never give the proper notice at closing. So, one could rescind every mortgage contract at foreclosure.

They give this option because one could have registered the note on a UCC, one would be the creditor anyway, so they can't foreclose. Rescission completely discharges the security agreement (the mortgage deed and the mortgage contract). One can ask for the entire amount of the mortgage note returned in the form of cash.

They should have given you the cash for your note at closing and closed the whole transaction without continuing payments. The house was paid for at closing with your negotiable instrument on one set of books. They didn't give you credit for the note because you didn't register the note and show a claim.

If you don't register the note, they will not give you your property back.

They can't give you the note back because they sold it. So, they should give all your payments back.

God has given us a prepaid account, so we never have to go into debt, if we are honorable. We should pay for everything with a promissory note.

An Antidote For Aphasia

All homes are legally abandoned because no one has made their claim for the money that was owed to them. One should have claimed the house at closing because the note paid it for. The bank has no claim. There is a third party that bought the note from the bank and holds an interest in the note. Foreclosure is damage, so they must give notice and the right to rescind. The notice of rescission is sent by certified mail. As soon as we do that, they try to claim that Reg. Z doesn't apply to residential mortgages. In the In Re: Maxwell case, the owner repeatedly asked for disclosure.

We used this case as a foundation for our case on the grounds that the mortgage transaction was an unconscionable act.

Whenever there is a lack of disclosure, one has an offset available. This is dangerous to the entire mortgage industry, however, a few cases are not going to cause a big problem. If most people want to be ignorant and be slaves to the banking system, they have the right to do that.

No attorney will make this type of claim because it jeopardizes the system that he works for. Nor was the attorney told what to do by the client.
Regulation Z shows the form in which the bank is required to give notice of rescission. They never give you notice in that form. They awarded the owner,
$595,000 in punitive and actual damages from the bank. Plus, they rescinded the contract.

They said the contract was unconscionable under UCC 2-302.
One also had the right to rescind if the property is on a flood plain that was not disclosed. Many new floodplains have been declared. The whole state of Ohio is surrounded by navigable waters under USC Title 33 and is a flood plain. Where the high-water mark goes, one is subject to admiralty maritime law providing Federal jurisdiction. It is caused a hazard area under **Title 42 USC 4012(a)**.

FEMA defines the flood plain. There was no flood insurance on the property when the loan was originated. It is not possible to take out a loan in a floodplain area without flood insurance. That voids the contract.

Affirmative Defense
The claim or affirmative defense is that this is another ground for rescission. They never disclosed that the property was in a flood hazard area and there was no flood hazard insurance. **That is a violation of UCC 3-407,** a material alteration to the original contract.

The government is trying to expand the definition of wetlands and floodplains. This is related to securitization in which they transform negotiable instruments into securities.

They move them from UCC article 3 to article 8.
Ohio code section 1707.01(b) a promissory note is defined as a security. So one can use rescission on it also. Under Ohio code 1707-261, one has the right to restitution and rescission when they sell an unregistered security. As soon as the bank gets your mortgage note, they sell it. Banks register mortgage deeds, not mortgage notes.

Lisa gave a note to the county to discharge her criminal case. The county likely deposited it in a bank and received a cash receipt. The bank likely sold it as an unregistered security. This provides Victoria with another remedy. But she needs to register it on a UCC3 before it can be used as a claim.

An Antidote For Aphasia

www.kahantazadaq.net
info@kahantazadaq.net

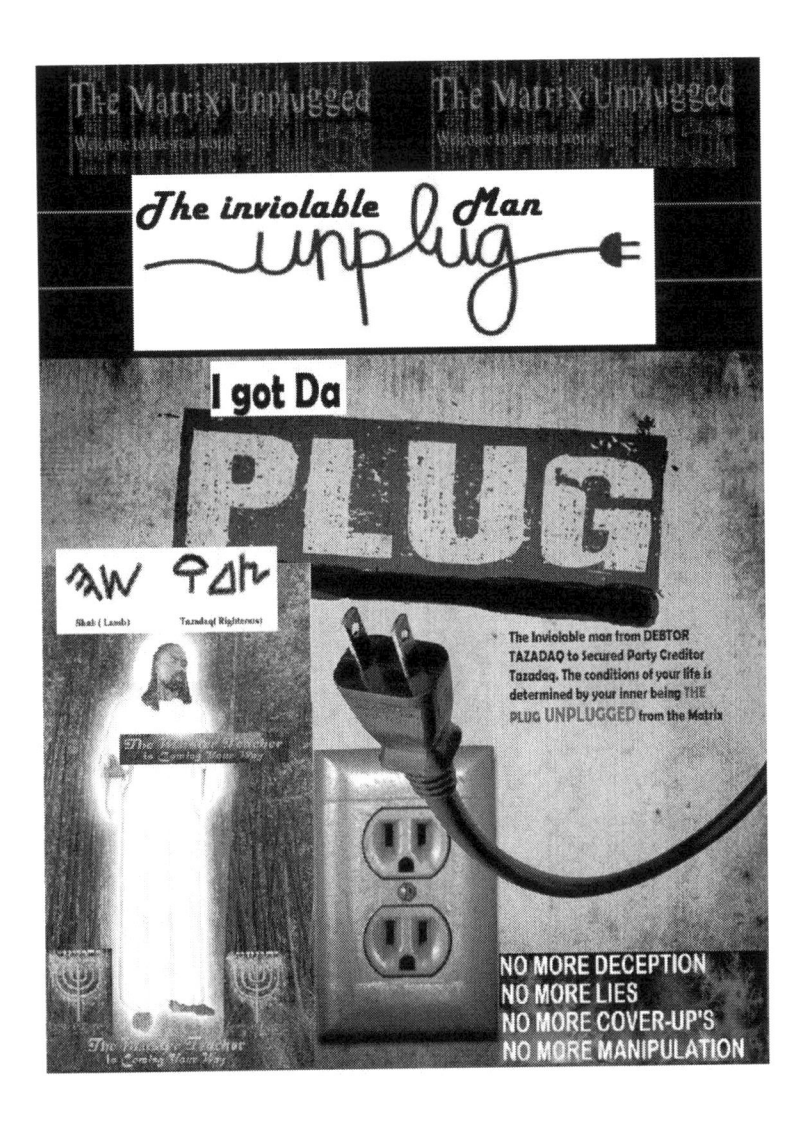

An Antidote For Aphasia

Order now @ www.kahantazadaq.net

9 SECURITIZATION III

Banks securitize mortgages by selling them to an SPV (a special purpose vehicle, a trust). Then they create bonds of trust assets to sell to DTC. The bank cannot foreclose on the note, because they are not a holder and lack standing.
However, the mortgage contract requires payments. This makes the note non-negotiable. They are foreclosing on the contract under common law, not the note. The bank claims to be a holder in due course, but that is not possible for there to be a holder in due course of a nonnegotiable instrument. Non-negotiable instruments are governed by common law, not the UCC.

SPV- A special purpose vehicle, an organization constructed for a limited purpose and life. Frequently these SPVs serve as conduits or pass through organizations or corporations about securitization. The entity that holds the legal rights over the asset transferred by the originator.
The originator of a mortgage is the living man. If he is the originator, the SPV becomes the legal holder when the deed is signed.
The bank is acting in the capacity of a servicer.
When you are involved in a foreclosure case, the strawman creates an illusion. No party is real.

So, the real parties in interest are not involved in the court. The bank may be named as the plaintiff on the foreclosure is the servicer. The real party in interest is the SPV.
Patriots usually ask the plaintiff to produce the note.
The note is not negotiable because it has terms and conditions associated with the instrument which could lead to a question as to whether the terms and conditions have been met. A negotiable instrument can have no restrictions, terms, or conditions.
One, the note is non-negotiable. Two, it is never registered to the public. These instruments cannot appear in court.

If it was brought into court, the judge would see that it is not registered, and would claim he has no subject matter jurisdiction over your claim.

Secondly, it is not negotiable, so it does not come under the UCC Negotiable Instruments Act. Consequently, it comes under contract obligations, so the appearance of the note is immaterial and irrelevant.

Especially since it was never registered to the public. The next problem is, since the note is not registered, what standing does the plaintiff, the bank, have there? Under the UCC, the plaintiff has no standing if he is not a holder in due course.

The plaintiff is not there on the note for several reasons. It also shows that the bank is liable, and the originator is the creditor. The note is an asset to the defendant, which is a counterclaim for recoupment. It does not support the bank's case.

Before closing the note goes into an SPV which now has legal title to these issues, and it creates a new instrument in the place of the note. They create securities and bonds, which are registered. The plaintiff is representing the registered security and bond at closing. They are hiding the pea under several shells, so you don't know where it is. This keeps the Patriots from making the proper claims.

Receding

The statute says you have a right to restitution and rescission if they sell an unregistered security, Ohio statute 1707-261. Is the note an unregistered security? It is a non-negotiable instrument. When they convert it into a security, it takes it out of UCC Article 3. It could be under UCC article 4 because it is deposited in a bank. But eventually, after it has gone into the SPV, and been securitized, it is moved to UCC Article 8 and Article 9 applies to the remedy. They must give you the right to rescission because it is unregistered.

So, they ledger that you no longer have a liability by giving you the setoff. So, they are following the law. But they are keeping the records in two different sets of books like The Mafia.

We are following the letter of the law and showing them what they are doing. We have a right to rescind and restitution, which is also part of recoupment. We can go to the NASD, the National Association of Securities Dealers, they have an arbitration and resolution board located in NYC. They have tribunals in each state for hearings. You can go to arbitration and have the contract rescinded and get restitution because they are selling unregistered securities. I have examples of four recent cases from 2005 and 2006. People have purchased promissory notes and found out they were unregistered securities. There is case law on this. This is money laundering or RICO.

But there is a statute protecting us. Since, as soon as they sell the unregistered security, we are entitled to set off to settle the claim. We are raising this claim; we have not waived it. They have not addressed our claims or defenses, so we have grounds for appeal. The law requires them to do this because they have raised it. One can stop any mortgage on this basis.

They would be better off if the judge gave you a remedy on other grounds. We have given them several grounds for rescission. They can also allow rescission because the property is in a flood plain. Their attorney said that if what we are saying is true, it would destroy the mortgage market. We had an attorney say the same in her pleadings fifteen years ago, and then she was taken off the case. I don't think they like attorneys saying those things in public.

Federal court throughout our RICO complaint initially. I brought up the FASB and IASB standards and regulations in appellate court. I corrected them by stating that the bank is the creditor. That is only true on the receivable side of the ledger. We are the creditors, and they are the debtors on the liability ledger. That provides a remedy.

The G7 has endorsed it. Now we are getting into international law, with the IASB standards that they have adopted. These standards say we have a right to set off.

So, like the Mafia, they always have a second set of books that are not available to the public. They only use the public books when they make a claim against us to determine how much we know about our claims available on the other side of the accounting. It is up to us to bring this claim or waive our remedy. Most CPAs are not familiar with these issues, because they don't have to deal with them.

Bank One uses KPMG to audit its books; others use Price Waterhouse. They are international auditing services. They are experts at auditing off-balance-sheet accounts. There is off-balance sheet financing, payables, and receivables. These auditors are the only ones that are aware of these issues. Scott Taub who was the chief accountant for the SEC and his assistant. They confirmed my information.

The SEC is also the enforcement agent for this practice because it involves securities. He admitted that this is their practice. He wanted to know who I was, but I did not tell him.

One bank auditor wanted to know why I was asking these questions. What does why I am asking have to do with the question? "Are going to tell me what you are going to do with my note? Don't I have a right to know what you are doing with my note if I go into business with you? "Everybody thinks a note is a liability, but it is not. Under UCC 4(a), 104(c), it says that the originator is the sender of the first fund transfer. We are the first funds transferor. **UCC 3-105(a)(c), subsection**
(a) talks about the issue, and (c) talks about the issuer. It defines the issuer as the transferor of the first fund transfer, which is the drawer and the maker.

☐
UCC 8-102 (12), (15) and (9) defined what an entitlement holder is.

UCC 8- 105 that says we are identified as the person with securities and entitlement rights on the books of a banking intermediary. They call them intermediaries under Article 8. This practice is all under Article 8 because it involves securities. That is how they are hiding their practices. They are treating these notes as securities and not Article 3 papers. Under Article 8 we are the holders of entitlement and possessory rights to the proceeds of the transaction because we are the originator of the first funds transfer on the accounts payable side of the ledger. We are entitled to the funds.

A promissory note is an asset to us. When we give it to a beneficiary and he deposits it, it becomes a cash item to the bank. They issue a cash receipt to the depositor. The bank gets a cash receipt that is the equivalent of money. It is what passes for money in society. They will tell us that our note is not cash. But after it is deposited it looks as if we deposited money in an account.

This is a cash proceed under Title 12 of the USC. We are the creditors, and we are not bringing this up as a defense. This is why there cannot be a holder in due course.
UCC 3-302 defines a holder in due course. It says in the first paragraph that in this section a holder in due course is subject to 3-106(d). That says that where an instrument is involved, there cannot be a holder in due course. The reason they can't is because they are taking it subject to the defenses and claims that the drawer and maker as the originator of the first funds transfer can bring against the payee, which is the bank. The reason there can't be a holder in due course is that we are the creditor, and we can trump any claim that a holder might have on that instrument.

The claim that the originator and maker can make is set off because they sold an unregistered note. They cannot be a holder in due course because they are taking it subject to administrative and commercial claims, every time there is a clause in the instrument. They create a mortgage purchase loan (16 CFR 433.1). This whole process is not about mortgages at all, because they sold the note received the funds, and closed the account by assuming they have repaid the originator on the loan. If they already repaid the originator on the loan, the living man who signed the note, then the whole thing is closed. We got our money back.

We did not receive the money or ask for the note back. So, the bank transaction on the payables side shows that we brought the money in, and they credited it to our account, so they paid it back, we don't have a claim against the bank. It stayed in the account because we didn't claim it. So, they assume it has been abandoned. A trustee of abandoned assets would normally invest these assets to make money on them. They are expecting rent for this property from us. We are not paying monthly payments of principal and interest, is because the loan has been paid off.

We are paying rent for the assets we failed to collect. The SPV is taking all the payments as profit. It is under contract and has nothing to do with notes and contracts it ends when the original contract is finished.

If you stop making payments, no one has been damaged. The only reason the banks continue to collect for 30 years is because you are a fool. We are responsible for agreeing to this contract. We don't have a fraud claim.

We did the first funds transfer that they transferred to the receivables as an asset to the bank. When they didn't give the note back, the bank sold it or deposited it as a cash item. UCC 1-204 says we are considered merchants at law, who know what we are doing. We act as though we are experts at negotiable instruments. That is how they get around the defense of fraud in the inducement.

To prove fraud in the inducement, one must prove he didn't know what they were doing and didn't have sufficient time to find out. But to prove that you must learn how to do it right first.

An Antidote For Aphasia

They call their process de-recognition. But most of the time that is not true. If they pass the reward and the risk, a complete sale of the asset, it is de-recognition.

De-recognition is defined in accounting as not recognizing it on their books anymore or removing it of the balance sheet. This means they extinguished the loan from the books. We are asking for the balance sheet in discovery. The balance sheet will show that the loan has been extinguished. They are trying to collect on a note that they have no right title or interest in.

Pimpco on Bonds, using the real estate is not the mortgage loan. It is used to securitize commodities and securities exchange. They are not using mortgages to attach property, because it only appears that they got an interest in attaching the property.

We have priority. Their real intent is to create derivatives to create a security and bond market to finance all commercial and corporate activity. Tying up the land is a profitable byproduct because nobody understands that they don't have a claim for it. They are called beneficial interest holders (BIHS). Those are the organizations with an account with the DTC to buy the mortgage-backed bonds, which are the pooled assets from the HELOC or trust.

There is no difference between a civil case, a criminal case or a mortgage deed and mortgage loan purchase. Victoria had a couple of traffic cases back in the early 1990s. Victoria was in jail for a while. She was jailed for six months in 2001 based on a personal complaint, but they discovered an old warrant for her arrest. She attempted to get the feds to prosecute the county under Title 42 because the judge had said that the warrants had expired. She settled and closed the probation with a note.

But she recently found an old warrant poster on her on the Internet.

An Antidote For Aphasia

She found out that a Hong Kong investment company purchased her criminal case bond. It is possible that she didn't have standing to ask for a Title 42 lawsuit, because she had not filed a bailee/bailor agreement and therefore, she was not a creditor.

One must be a creditor to make a claim. Everyone today is presumed to be an enemy of the state, a U.S. citizen. This game is played in admiralty maritime commercial law. When you file a UCC1 bailor/bailee you are saying that you want to be a creditor. A creditor in an admiralty transaction is the same as a sovereign with inalienable rights in common law. It is a way of colorable stating that I must stand as a creditor to get a remedy.

An Antidote For Aphasia

10 YOU ARE THE CREDITOR IN THEIR PAYABLES BOOKS

You are the creditor in their payable books. As a slave, you can only plead guilty. But without the UCC1, you didn't have any documents to show that you could come in as the creditor on the liability account of the corporation. If you can come in where the defacto government owes you instead of having the defacto government claim you owe them, you have a counterclaim for a set-off.

Moors want to use Nationality, and Patriots want to use the common law, but the government is focusing on you as a debtor by a voluntary contract of servitude. The government treats you like a slave unless you know enough to understand how a slave can pay off his debt and get his liberty and freedom.

They are speaking in a different language, so we don't understand, asking for our liberty presuming we don't have a debt. We languish in a foreign jail because we cannot understand the remedy.

How do I get them to acknowledge this so I can come in with standing as a creditor? Do I send a precipe to the clerk seeking his acknowledgment and his appointment of this attorney? She has not received an answer from the Secretary of State of Puerto Rico acknowledging her filing. If there is no filing number, what document do I have to show there is a B/B agreement to give me standing in the court to direct the Title 42 action to appoint an attorney to go after the state for its unlawful actions against the strawman because they didn't have a valid warrant.

An Antidote For Aphasia

Once you do your B/B filing showing the relationship, then you can bring that document in. Just like the collateral being the note in a foreclosure case, the collateral in the criminal case has to be our signature on the note that we gave them in the criminal case for the settlement and closure. That is your claim in that criminal case. The note we gave the bank was the claim in the foreclosure case. That is your asset. One should not put the indictment in the collateral on the UCC, because it is a liability to you and an asset to the corporation. It is their account receivable. The IBOE that you sent them is your asset and it constitutes your claim.

Victoria gave them an IBOE to settle the case. They have not returned the note or settled the account. This is just like a bank mortgage. The mortgage deed is still recorded after you gave them the note. But when you gave them the note, they closed the account. But then they sold the note for other investments to other corporations off the balance sheet in the background. How can you show them that you have an ongoing interest in that note to settle that account? Have you been making monthly payments to show an ongoing interest in the note?

For example: you purchased real estate. They give you a deed. They recorded the deed. You got the mortgage deed; you got the mortgage note and you got the mortgage contract. The mortgage deed is superimposed on top of the deed. The mortgage deed has priority because it was filed last, and it is sequenced with the same party that is on the deed. The public looks at the mortgage deed and it appears to be a legal, lien hold interest in the property. It is not a negotiable note.

A Federal Reserve note is a negotiable note that is registered as a security. So the FRN passes in public. If you deposit an FRN with a deposit slip in the bank, the bank accepts the deposit as a cash item, and they give you a cash receipt. They do not do that when you give them your note, because it is non-negotiable and not registered in the public. So, the transaction does not appear on the public side of the books because there is no public registration.

It does appear on the private side of the account because the note is private. When your note comes into the bank, they offset the private side of the account, but they can't offset the public side because it isn't registered. So, it cannot appear in the public side to offset the public side of the accounting.

We use monthly payments to show the public that we have an interest in that property. The legal title to the note has been transferred to the SPV. So, you no longer have legal title to the property. We must use the monthly payments to show we have a claim to the property because it was our note. We make monthly payments on the mortgage and the utilities and yearly payments on taxes. If we were not paying those, we would have no receipts to show that we had any continuing interest in the property.

If we filed an interest in the property as a creditor, we would not have to make all those monthly payments on the property. We can choose to be a creditor or debtor. But if you are a debtor and stop making payments, the presumption will be that you are abandoning your interest in the property for possession and use. You already abandoned the legal title. The bank can step in and take over because of another level of abandonment

when the mortgage deed is still recorded in the register but when you gave them the note they closed out the account. Then they sold the note for other investments to other corporations off the balance sheet in the background. How do they prove that you have an ongoing interest in that note that you gave them to settle that account? That is why you make monthly payments on that note that you abandoned to show that you have an ongoing interest.

An Antidote For Aphasia

Yahusha is the Social Security Number For Yahuah

You must provide an application with a name, address, and SSN to sign up for a utility on the property. The SSN is the prepaid trust account. So, you sign up for your utilities with your prepaid account. Within 30 days, instead of giving them a BOE on the prepaid account, you keep coming in with liability notes to keep showing a debtor interest rather than a prepaid interest on the account because you failed to register.

The application for the utilities is the equivalent of signing a negotiable instrument or a private note because your unrestricted signature with the account name and number is equivalent authority for the utility to keep drawing off your prepaid account to run their corporate utility business. You show a continuing monthly interest by your bill paying with liability notes. If you try to pay with a BOE, you should register the original contract you signed because that is the equivalent of unlimited credit access to the prepaid account. That is your asset in that transaction. If it is not registered, you can't show that the public should settle the public side of that accounting. If you send them a BOE that is unregistered, they will not accept it. They cannot see any public side of your BOE.

Lisa has not been making monthly payments and she put the three criminal cases on a UCC filing. The BOE that you gave them in the criminal case is collateral. The case is not an asset; the case is a forum to settle the transaction. The note should be put on the UCC. The criminal case is not settled because you have not made a claim. You have not put the note as collateral on the UCC.

You are like a person in a mortgage foreclosure case who stops making payments and has not shown a continuing interest in the property by any filing in the public. Monthly payments would have been a monthly filing of a notice of interest. A notice of interest will expire if you don't renew it. The bank is foreclosing on you for presumed abandonment of the property.

An Antidote For Aphasia

You didn't record your assets, which is your mortgage note that you gave them to begin with. The mortgage note is an asset to you and a liability to the bank and you didn't record the note, to make it a security registered with the public. Therefore, it is not cognizable by the public court system to give you a remedy when the bank did not close the full accounting with you at your escrow closing when you brought the property and when the note was closed off the bank's books on their liability side, you have no public claim.

How can you claim the note as an asset when you give it to them? The note is an asset, like a lawnmower. If you give it to somebody, they owe you something back. You are the creditor in the transaction. You were the originator of the transaction. When you buy a house, you sign a mortgage note to the bank. You are the creditor. Did you give the court a BOE to settle the account in the current case?

That was an original instrument therefore you are the creditor. They owe you a receipt or a canceled check. Like Roger Elvick used to say, you should receive a check. They didn't give the BOE back to you, because first, they closed the account on one side otherwise they would be involved in fraud. But you didn't ask for the note back and they presume you didn't make a claim, it is a valuable asset, so they sell it to someone else. So someone else has a claim on that note that Vic used to settle her criminal case. Somebody is holding it. They bought it from the state.

But they closed your account, the charges in criminal court; but only on one side. The case isn't settled because they haven't applied the funds from the note to the other side. They have not given you credit for your assets or your liability to close the full account. You have not made a claim.

The receivables side is still open because the note does not show any public registration. They closed the private side that you gave them the note for, but you didn't get it back, because you didn't claim it so therefore, they sold it again. So, they are still trying to collect the receivables, they sold her assets to another company that holds her asset, so she doesn't hold it and they are using the asset to create even more funding to run the corporations with.

This is because they didn't ask them to give the note back and you didn't show that you have a public claim. You can ask the bank all you want to give your note back. The bank is not going to listen to you, because they assume that you are a debtor, and they have no document of standing to show you are a creditor to ask for the note back. If we had registered it, we could certify it out of a public office, which they are required to accept.

Just like you told the lady in the foreclosure suit, put the note that you gave to the bank that they are using in the foreclosure, as collateral on the UCC filing. When she showed the filing to the judge, it showed I have a continuing public interest in the property. If you are not making the monthly payments, you have to have an instrument that shows you are still claiming the property. I am a creditor; I have this UCC lien. It shows that I am a creditor with the property as collateral. I am the highest-level creditor on the property. The judge said, "Ok, it looks like you have priority."

The reason they still have a wanted sign for Victoria is because you gave them the note, they settled the private side, so she doesn't owe them any more for the crime. They settled on the private side, they didn't give her the note back, we held it, and she didn't show she had a claim to get it, but we have settled the substance of the criminal charges. So, they settled into the one side which is their liability side, which means they don't owe her anymore, which means they recognize the substance of what she gave them.

But if they gave it back to her, none of the rest of the transactions could continue, because everything is based on her credit line. So they had to create a presumption that they didn't have to give it back to her. One, she doesn't have a registration that shows she is a creditor and because it isn't registered, we can't close out the public side. Since we can't close out the public side, we may as well not give her note back and we will sell that note to another corporate entity that can use it again anyway because she doesn't know to ask for it.

They closed one side just like the bank did the mortgage at closing in escrow. They don't want to hold any money anymore. This whole thing is done, but she never came and asked for her money with standing, ie, the note that got canceled, so consequently we will sell this liability to some other corporation as their asset. Now you have the right to claim that you are the ultimate claim on the closing of the criminal account. I want the case settled and I want the wanted poster down.

They cannot take the wanted poster down yet, because there is a silent party in the background that holds the note. You don't hold it. Someone else holds it, so someone else has a claim, an account ready for collection as a creditor. The company in Hong Kong that bought the accounts receivable is the creditor with a claim in this case. The wanted poster is still up to show the investor's public interest in Victoria to give public notice that they have a claim.

If you don't show a public interest that you have a claim, you have abandoned it and they are going to come in for collection in court. If Vic isn't making the probation monthly reports, the Hong Kong company will bring her in. They are not going to show up in court. The county will show up in court to press charges as the servicing bank on the account that was purchased by an SPV. The SPV is the conduit to funnel the money to the Hong Kong investment corporation. But the investor is the true moving

Edgar Bradley was on federal probation in which he tendered a note to settle and close. Ed kept telling them he was the creditor, why haven't you closed the account? The probation officer reported to the court that Bradley was not meeting the monthly probation requirements and asked to revoke his parole. He was brought in briefly to a magistrate in who they adopted the recommendation of the parole office and he was going to submit it to the judge. At that point, he had the opportunity to rebut and do affirmative defenses or counterclaims.

The judge agreed with the magistrate and told Bradley to report back to federal prison for three months because of parole violations.
☐   Edgar Bradley had already sent an IBOE to the feds to settle and close the account. He had not registered for his BOE. So he failed to make a claim. So they settled the private side, but because he couldn't show standing they did not settle the public side of the account. Since they couldn't settle the receivable side, they had to sell it to a foreign investor to avoid fraud. When they canceled the probation, the new investor in the background was the moving party.

I assume that they put him in for 90 days to see if anyone was going to prove a claim. When nobody proved the claim, they let him out again, with three more years of probation. This is likely the security to protect the investment interest of the purchaser of the public account receivable. This is caused by the failure to register the note and file a security interest in the public sector to settle and close the account.

Admiralty Maritime only has authority for execution of sentences for contempt for failure to pay a debt. He did not record his notes in the public so the accountants can settle their claims.
There is another guy in a similar situation as Pete with the state tax authorities. The state hired an attorney to collect the accounts receivable after he tendered a BOE. The state needed to sell the account because Pete gave them the substance for closing. But Pete is in contempt because Pete did not register his instrument to allow the account to settle and close.

Therefore, the punishment is to sell the account to a third-party investor for collection. They have to put up some notice of interest to protect the investor, which will appear to interfere with your rights and privileges as punishment for you for not allowing us to settle the account. They are not punishing anyone for violating the law. They are not concerned about monthly payments.

They cannot take the wanted poster down because there is a silent party in the background that holds the note. The wanted poster is the collateral they are using to support their claim. If you want the poster taken down, settle the claim. They can make a claim with an unregistered security, but they don't have a defense if you bring a registered claim. That is why they are not picking you up, so that you will not make that claim. Your claim will close that account down. They want that investor to keep it open and enjoy the return. They won't pick you up but they have public notice of interest. Notice of interest does not have to be proven unless there is a claim against it.

Lisa has been trying to buy a house in Australia, but it hasn't settled and closed yet, because she hasn't registered the payment to the public. She is concerned about a bad credit rating. They give you bad credit ratings when you don't pay your bills because you don't know how the system works.

No one in the USA should have a bad credit rating because they have a prepaid account and Can purchase Kahan Tazadaq's nooks wipe Your Credit Clean Now.

Order books and apparel @ www.kahantazadaq.net

Why You Pay Property Tax: and How With Draw

Debtors paying property tax is one of those things that most United States citizens have accepted as if it were a way of life. However, most debtors are unaware as to why they pay property tax in the first place. If Debtors knew why they paid this tax, they could then choose whether or not to pay it, because like all taxes in this country, the property tax is not mandatory.

If you knew the truth, would you continue to pay? Most debtors will say that property tax goes to support education, and if you don't pay the property tax then you don't care anything about educating our children. This is the cry of all good Debtor socialists, the enemies of Americanism and the principles of limited government and natural rights. Anyone who has researched the educational system even a little knows that the United States Department of Education has based its system on the Soviet education system.

This was proven by former Senior member of Ronald Reagan's Department of Education, a courageous woman who surreptitiously removed documents, and then exposed the truth for all to know. Let's get back to the argument made by Debtor socialists concerning how property tax money is used for education, and if you don't pay it then you are against education. Kahan Tazadaq contends that money is the fuel for bureaucracies.

When a system (like education) is failing to properly educate our children, but rather is making them into mindless, unthinking, docile, and obedient servants of government, effectively slaves for the just over-broke workforce, then by fueling the system you are simply guaranteeing that it will continue to do what it is doing. If the results of the current system are undesirable, then stop giving it fuel and it will cease to operate. Now that we have dealt with the principal naysayers, let's talk about the property tax itself. There are only two kinds of taxes - direct and indirect. Direct taxes are prohibited by the Constitution - not once but twice. Direct taxes are taxes on that which you already own, and there may be no direct taxes under any circumstances short of a state of war, and then only if the taxes are equally apportioned among the Union states. Apportionment works like this: say the United States government wants to raise 500 million dollars for the " Iran war effort."

Say, too, that Texas has ten (10%) percent of the population. California gets a bill for 50 million dollars. Now let's say that Texas has 25 million people at this time. Everybody pays two dollars. That's apportionment. It does not consider how much or how little you earn, how much or how little you have, etc., it is completely fair and equable. An apportioned tax must be repealed within two years of its enactment.

The other type of tax is the indirect tax. Indirect taxes are taxes on a particular activity, or taxes levied at the point of purchase. If you do not want to pay the tax, don't engage in the taxed activity or don't purchase the taxed item.

Lawfully avoiding indirect taxes is easy. America was established so that a Citizen need not ever pay any tax unless he wished to do so. So, what is the property tax? Property Taxes are an indirect tax, levied because you have voluntarily used government services, and also because your property has been classified as a commercial piece of property. Show Kahan Tazadaq the law requiring a real property owner to record his property with the County Recorder if your debtors don't believe me. Go ask your Recorder or County Counsel.

Therefore, when you do record your property, you are using government services that you are not required to use. Your property tax goes to pay for those services. When you record your property, you enter a Trustor/Trustee relationship, in which your real property has been transferred into a government trust, and you are given authorized permission to use their property (warranty deed). Further, your property tax is based on a commercial classification that has been assigned to your real property.

I guarantee you that your property has been classified as agricultural, industrial, or residential. Each of these is commercial (the legal definition of "resident" is a class of government official; residential is a house in which a government official lives). There are three ways to lawfully withdraw out of property taxes: obtain allodial title, unrecord your property, or have your real property re-classified as private. If you want to know how to Donate $30 now on cash.me/$tazadaqshah or on Zelle @ tazadoctrine@gmail.com or on PayPal.me/tazadaq

The allodial title means supreme ownership. In the united States of America, all property is allodial. This means that all property is subject to supreme ownership by the people. This also means that federal government activities which take private or public land to use for environmental or biosphere purposes are illegally stolen from the people, who are their rightful owners.

If you can obtain allodial title to your real property, you will have effectively created an envelope in which you reign supreme (e.g. the King has allodial title to the castle and the kingdom). No zoning ordinances, easements, bureaucratic regulations, or state or federal law have any effect on property held in Allodium.

You have created a kingdom amid bureaucratic chaos, and you will never again receive any property tax assessments. The government does not want you to obtain allodial title to your property. The allodial title means supreme ownership. In the united States of America, all property is allodial.

There are three main steps toward acquiring an allodial title. First, the property must be completely paid off. No mortgage, lien, or other attachment can exist.

Second, you must go to the County Recorder and do a title search. Do it yourself; do not have an attorney (vested interest) or title company representative do it for you, because nobody has as much interest as you in the results

Search for yourself. You must search back to the original land grants, ensuring that there are no hidden clouds on the title. Once you have completed a successful title search, file for a federal land patent on the land on which the property is located (if the property is in one of the original thirteen states, you will need to go to the state for a land patent no federal land patents exist for these states). Now comes the hardest part. Every piece of recorded real property is used to collateralize government loans, so your real property has public debt attached to it. You need to find out the amount of the public debt (approximately seven times the annual property tax) and the holder of the debt, and then pay it off.

An Antidote For Aphasia

The government doesn't want you to accomplish this, so they will work against you. I suggest you burn the research candle at both ends, so to speak. Contact the County Recorder in the county where the property is located. Contact the Department of the Interior in Washington, D.C. Be prepared in both instances to meet with clerks who do not know what you are talking about. Ask for supervisors until you get someone who can help you.

The process of un-recording your property is easier, though not quite as solid. It is since you are assessed a tax based upon using government services (County Recorder) to which you are not entitled or mandated. The process involves transferring ownership to another party, notifying the County Recorder that a transfer has been completed, and then having the property after a reasonable time has passed, transferred back into your name.

If done correctly, the property is not recorded anymore, and there will be no further tax assessments. A man in New York had 160 acres and wanted to give two of them to his son. He called the Tax Assessor and asked him to reduce his assessment to 158 acres. The Assessor did so. The son never recorded his two acres.

Twelve and a half years passed. The son now wanted to borrow money on his two acres. The bank said they would loan him the money, but only if he recorded the property first. He wanted the money, so he recorded the property. Two weeks later, he received a property tax statement, for the current year only! The past twelve years went un-assessed, no tax!

If you want to pursue this option, I suggest you visit www.kahantazadaq,net and order the plug and the Infliction of Commerce. Help@kahantazadaq.net 347-618-1783a very good guaranteed program that will help you to do this.

The final method of withdrawing from property tax is one that I developed a couple of years ago. It involves the classification of property on which the assessed tax is based. Property that is taxed is always identified by one of three commercial classifications: residential, industrial, or agricultural.

Private property cannot be taxed. Contact your Tax Assessor and ask for a written explanation of the numbered codes appearing on your property tax statement. Once you have deciphered the statement, you will find your property classified by one of the above commercial designations. Write a letter to your Tax Assessor, explaining that you have discovered an error in your tax statement.

Do not mention the tax itself, as the error in question relates only to the classification. Explain that your property has mistakenly been classified as _____ (agricultural, industrial, residential), and please correct the classification to read "private." Ask the Assessor to notify you by mail once the matter has been handled. Be polite and sign the letter, using words like "Sincerely", "Best wishes", etc.

There is no reason to be belligerent at this point. If the Assessor honors your wishes, you will never see a property tax statement again. If, as is more likely, the Assessor writes back, refusing to adjust his records, you may now open up a discussion as to why not. Ask whether you have the right to own private property. He will say yes, of course. Ask why he refuses to classify it as private property.

He will either explain to you that he cannot tax property unless it is classified pursuant to constitutional limitations (residential, industrial, agricultural), or he will reveal to you that you do not own the property (in which case he has admitted to fraud, nullifying the transfer of property in the first place, since you were not aware of what you were doing at the time). In either case, once the Assessor brings up taxation, you can now make the argument that your real property has been re-classified, without your permission, for the sole purpose of taxation. This is the firm basis for a lawsuit. There is a Tax Assessor (not a clerk, the actual Assessor) in Tennessee who has admitted that he cannot tax private property. He can, if necessary, be subpoenaed to testify. There is a private Citizen

en in Tennessee, who has not received a penny in property tax assessments on his private land (160 acres or so) for over fifteen years! If you need it for a court case, he will sign an affidavit so stating. In other words, the precedent exists, and therefore, if you pursue it, you cannot lose! This method is relatively new, so it has little track record. However, it is based upon sound law, and I invite you to try it out on your real property.

Remember, in the united States of America, each Citizen has the right to live his/her life without paying any taxes at all! All taxes are voluntary! Learn why you pay taxes, and you can learn how to stop paying them. And for those who insist that you are somehow hurting people by not paying taxes to the government when the government starts living within the limitations which We the People have imposed on them; when they stop violating our natural rights and show that they can be trusted with the powers

We the People have granted them when they stop trying to force us to pay for their socialist, un-American programs, then we will consider whether they are worthy of receiving a portion of the fruit of our labor. Until then, I say let the government starve.

When Is the Shabbat?

(1): The first scripture we would like to begin with is {Gen 2:1-3}: – The heavens and earth were finished, and all the host of them. On the Seventh Day The Most High ended his work; He rested on the Seventh Day from all His work which he had made. The Most High Blessed the Seventh Day and sanctified it. He rested from all his work which the Most High created and made. These verses show the beginning of the Most High's first instituted Sabbath.

(2):The next scripture is {Exodus 20:8-11}: - (8th verse) – Remember the Sabbath Day, to keep it holy (9th verse) – Six days shalt thou labour and do all thy work: (10th verse) – But the Seventh Day is the Sabbath of the Lord Most High; in it thou shalt not do any work, thou, nor thy son, nor the daughter, thy manservant, nor thy maidservant; nor the cattle, nor thy stranger that is within thy gates: (11th verse) – For in Six Days The Most High made heaven and earth, the sea, and all that in them is and rested the Seventh Day; wherefore The Most High blessed the Sabbath Day and hallowed it.

In these verses The Most High is saying remember The Sabbath Day (Friday sundown to Saturday sundown) the Seventh Day of the week. The Most High rested on the Seventh Day, blessed and hallowed the Sabbath (meaning made it holy and sanctified the Seventh Day which is The Sabbath).

(3): The next scripture is {Isaiah 58:13-14} (13th verse) – If thou turn away the foot from The Sabbath, (NOT SUNDAY) from during thy pleasure on my holy day; and call the Sabbath a delight, thy holy of The Most High, honorable; and shalt honor him, not doing thine own ways, nor finding thine own pleasure, nor speaking thine own words: In this 13th verse The Most High is showing the observance of The Sabbath, and if one turns away his path from The Most High's Sabbath, and doing your pleasure on his Holy Day. (The first instituted High Holy Day) doing your own way, finding your pleasure (shopping, buying, having sex, playing sports etc.,) or speaking your own words (foolish talk, gesturing, foul words or profane talking).

14th verse – Then shalt thou delight thyself in The Most High; and I will cause thee to ride upon The High places of the earth and feed thee with the heritage of Jacob thy father: for the mouth of The Most High hath spoken it. The Most High is saying through Isaiah the prophet, if his people Israel delight themselves in The Most High Sabbath, by keeping it, he will cause them to ride upon the high places of the earth and will feed them with the heritage of their father Jacob (spiritual and physical blessings, health, finances).

(4): The next scripture is {Isaiah 66:22-24} - (22nd verse) - For as the new heavens and the new earth, which I will make, shall remain before me saith The Most High, so shall your seed and your name remain. In the coming future kingdom of The Most High, where there is a new heavens and earth (rulership, a new and cleaned-up environment free from pollution hazardous waste, toxic waste chemical waste nuclear waste and a depleted ozone layer). The seed represents our generation or offspring. Our name represents, the name Hebrew Israelites restored as the original descendants of ancient biblical Israel.

(23rd verse) - And they shall go forth and look upon the carcasses of the men that have transgressed against me: for their worm shall not die, neither shall their fire be quenched; and they shall be an abhorring unto all flesh. So all the people that have transgressed The Most High's Sabbath and his commandments, shall have their place in the Lake of Fire. The worm represents the maggots from the carcass (dead body) this will be a witness to all those that refuse, rejects or changes the Sabbath to Sunday, their fire will not be put out.

(5): The next scripture is {Luke 4:16-20/31-32} - (16th verse) - And he came to Nazareth, where he had been brought up: and, as his custom was, he went into the synagogue on The Sabbath Day and stood up for the read. In this very verse we see the Messiah keeping and observance of the Sabbath Day in the synagogue. If the Messiah kept the Sabbath, shouldn't all Churches be keeping the Sabbath (Friday sundown to Saturday sundown) as I'm writing and speaking this day and age?

(17th verse) - And there was delivered unto him the book of the prophet Isaiah. And when he had opened the book, he found the place where it was written, (18th verse) - The spirit of The Most High is upon me, because he hath anointed me to preach the gospel to the poor; he hath sent me to heal the broken hearted, to preach deliverance to the captives, and recovering of sight to the blind, to set at liberty them that are bruised, (19th verse) To preach the acceptable year of The Most High. (20th verse) And he closed the book, and he gave ti again to the minster, and sat down, and the eyes of all them that were in the synagogue were fastened on him. (31st verse) And came down to Caper'an-um, a city of Galilee, and taught them on the Sabbath Days.

As we see in the holy scripture the Messiah Yahusha taught on the Sabbath Days, which is a commandment to keep observe and worship The Most High. (32nd verse) And they were astonished at his doctrine: For his word was with power. When we search the holy scriptures The Most High never gave names to the days of the week, nor to the months of the year. The names of the days of the week, and months of the year came after the Babylonian captivity of Israel. The Most High called the weeks and months by number. Example: The first month, second month, twelve months. Example: The first day, second day, and the seventh day (Sabbath) Numbers 1:1, Leviticus 23:5-8, Exodus 12:1-3. The Bible makes the Sabbath the last day of the week. Yet through extra-biblical sources it is

possible to determine that the Sabbath at the time of (Messiah Ya-Ha-Wa-Shi) corresponds to our current _Saturday_. Therefore, it is common Israelite and Christian practice to regard Sunday as the first day of the week. (source of information gotten from internet: History

Information The Days of Week: http://webexhibits.org/calendars/week.html) It was Constantine The Great a pagan worshiper claiming he converted to Christianity, that changed the Seventh Day (Sabbath) to Sunday as being the Sabbath. That's the reason why the majority of these churches throughout the entire earth celebrate and observe Sunday as the Sabbath Day. {Daniel 7:25} - And he shall speak great words against The Most High, and think to change times and laws, and they shall be given into his hand until a time and times and the dividing of time. (source of information The History of Constantine the Great Conversion to Christianity internet or any major history books.

(6) The next scripture is {Matthew 28:1} - (1st verse) - In the end of the Sabbath, as it began to dawn toward the First Day of the week, (Sunday) came Mary Magdalene and the other Mary to see the sepulcher. The holy scriptures show us that Saturday is the Sabbath, and Sunday is the First Day of the week NOT the day of worship nor Sabbath. The resurrection and the Sabbath are two different events. The resurrection has nothing to do with the Messiah changing the Sabbath (Saturday) to Sunday. The Messiah DID NOT come to

change the Sabbath nor The Law of The Most High.

{Matthew 5:17-20} - Think not that I come to destroy (Abolish) The Law, or the prophets; I do not come to destroy, but to fulfill. (18th verse) - For verily I say unto you. Till heaven and earth pass, one jot or one title shall in no wise pass from the law, till all be fulfilled. (19th verse) Whosoever therefore shall break one of these least commandments and shall teach men so. He shall be called the least in the Kingdom of Heaven; but whosoever shall do and teach them, the same shall be called great in the Kingdom of Heaven. (20th verse) - For I say unto you, that except your righteousness shall exceed the righteousness of the Scribes and Pharisees, ye shall in no case enter the Kingdom of Heaven.

{Luke 16:17} - And it is easier for heaven and earth to pass, than one title of the law to fail. So, what The Master is saying is I did not change or destroy the Sabbath Day (Friday sundown to Saturday sundown) nor the LAW. And if any man or woman thinks or believes that he or she is in great trouble "Shalam"

(7) The next scripture is {Mark 16:1-2} (1st verse) - And when the Sabbath was past, Mary Magdalene, and Mary the mother of James, and Salome had brought sweet spices, that they might come and anoint him. (2nd verse) And very early in the morning, the First Day of the week, they came unto the sepulcher at the rising of the sun.

(8) The next scripture is Acts 13:14,15 & 27 & 42-44 - As we go through the Book of Acts, the Apostles and Paul (His Greek Name) his Israelite name is Saul, were keeping and observing the Sabbath Days a custom, commandment and law of The Most High. These areas where Paul were located, such as Iconium, Pisidia, Lystra, Macedonia, Philip, Thy-atira, Thessalonica, Corinth, and Ephesus. These are areas located in Asia Minor (present-day Turkey) and the areas of Greece and parts of Europe. So Saul traveled to these areas, from Jerusalem to teach and inform the Christians (who were and will always be Israelites). And also, the natural Gentiles (Europeans).

An Antidote For Aphasia

Acts 9:15-17.

Now the next scripture is Acts 16:11-15 - (11th verse) Therefore loosing from Tro'as, we came with a straight course to Samo-Thracia, and the next day to Ne-polis; (12th verse) - And from Thense to Philippi, which is the chief city of the part of Macedonia, (Greece) and a colony: and we were in that city abiding certain days. They were abiding certain days, but when we get to the next verse, we will see a clear example, that they kept the (Sabbath Friday Sunday to Saturday sundown) NOT SUNDAY the first day of the week to worship or serve The Most High.

Yahusha (Jesus Christ) kept the Sabbath why don't so-called modern Christians? The truth will make you mad, question your sincerity in Yahuah/God, and sit you free.

To those who refuse to acknowledge Yah's (God's) Sabbath it just shows what a hypocrite that you are. You are not God. No man has a right to change what God ordains. I did not say to worship on Saturday God did. Most of you churchgoers do not keep God's laws, you follow the doctrine of the world.

Justify with the bible why you worship on Sunday, you can't do it! So which God are you following? Not the one of the Bible, you follow a God given to you your slave master. Therefore, most of you need a revolution of your minds, "complete constructive change".

The Sabbath was instituted by God's own example on the seventh day of creation week.
" And on the seventh day, God ended his work which He had made; and he rested on the seventh day from all his work which He had made. And God blessed the seventh day and sanctified it; because that in it he had rested from all his work which God created and made" (Genesis 2:2-3). From this, we learn that it is the Shabbat over the Most High not man. How significant!

An Antidote For Aphasia

The very God of the universe chose to cease His labor-not because He was tired (Isaiah 40:28), but because He wanted to set an example for all mankind. He specifically blessed and made holy the seventh day as a Sabbath, a day of ceasing, well over two millennia before the time of Moses and the Old Covenant. Exodus 20:11 corroborates this fact:

Throughout His earthly ministry, Christ observed the Sabbath. Luke records:

"And he came to Nazareth, where he had been brought up: and, as his custom was, he went into the synagogue on the Sabbath day, and stood up for to read" (Luke 4:16).

Jesus was indeed Lord of the Sabbath; He was there in the beginning with God in creating it (John 1:3; Ephesians 3:9; Colossians 1:16; Hebrews 1: 1-2). He showed by His example how it was to be kept as a blessing for mankind, as a day of freedom and delight. He showed that doing good, taking care of animals, handling emergencies, and shelling out grain to eat, were all permissible on this day of rest (Matthew 12:11-12; Luke 14:5). He objected to the inhumane traditions of men that turned the Sabbath into a burden, but He upheld the rest, the rejuvenation, the freedom enjoined by the Fourth Commandment (Mark 3:1-5; Luke 13:11-17).

Even at the end of His ministry, a few days before He died to pay for the sins of the world, Jesus indicated that the Sabbath command would continue after His death. In prophesying the destruction that was to come to Jerusalem in A.D. 70, Jesus told His followers,

" But pray ye that your flight is not in the winter, neither on the Sabbath day" (Matthew 24:20).

"...rested the Sabbath day according to the commandment" (Luke 23:56).

History reveals that it was because of political and social pressures that the Sabbath was gradually abandoned for Sunday - long after the time of the Apostles. Severe anti-Jewish attitudes developed in the

An Antidote For Aphasia

Roman world during the first and second centuries. As acts of repression, the Romans outlawed circumcision, sacrificing, Sabbath keeping and other Jewish practices.

Consequently, Christians, particularly at Rome, found it expedient to put as much distance as possible between themselves and the Jews, to demonstrate to the Romans that they were not Jewish. One way they did this was to work on the Sabbath. Sunday, which was already used by many Romans as a holiday, was a convenient substitute. For a detailed account of this substitution, see the book From Sabbath to Sunday by Samuele Bacchiocchi (Gregorian Pontifical University Press, 1974).

When Constantine officially recognized Christianity in the fourth century, he put the power of the empire

For in six days the Lord made heaven and earth, the sea, and all that in them is, and rested the seventh day: Therefore, the Lord blessed the Sabbath day, and hallowed it."
"Remember the Sabbath day, to keep it holy. Six days shalt thou labour and do all thy work: But the seventh day is the Sabbath of the Lord thy God: in it thou shalt not do any work..." (Exodus 20:8- 10).

The importance of the Ten Commandments is shown by the fact that God gave them with His own voice and "inscribed them in stone with His own finger. He must have chosen very carefully the ten spiritual precepts to be included in this law, which was to serve as a constitution of sorts for the nation of Israel. Keep in mind, these were not new laws, they all go back to Creation, though they probably were not codified as Ten Commandments. For example, murder, lying, and adultery are all condemned from the beginning (Genesis 4:8-16; 20:3-6; 39:9; cf.

Romans 5:12-14). And as we've already seen, the Sabbath originated at Creation. Very possibly the Israelites did not observe it while they were slaves in Egypt, but when God gave them the Fourth

Commandment, He was not introducing some new law. He'd begun reminding them of the Sabbath some weeks earlier when He sent the manna only six days each week (Exodus 16).

Throughout His earthly ministry, Jesus observed the Sabbath. Luke records: "And he came to Nazareth, where he had been brought up: and, as his custom was, he went into the synagogue on the Sabbath day, and stood up for to read" (Luke 4:16).

Throughout His earthly ministry, Jesus observed the Sabbath. Luke records: "And he came to Nazareth, where he had been brought up: and, as his custom was, he went into the synagogue on the Sabbath day, and stood up for to read" (Luke 4:16).

Jesus was indeed Lord of the Sabbath; He was there in the beginning with God in creating it (John 1:3; Ephesians 3:9; Colossians 1:16; Hebrews 1: 1-2). He showed by His example how it was to be kept as a blessing for mankind, as a day of freedom and delight. He showed that doing good, taking care of animals, handling emergencies, shelling out grain to eat, were all permissible on this day of rest (Matthew 12:11-12; Luke 14:5). He objected to the inhumane traditions of men that turned the Sabbath into a burden, but He upheld the rest, the rejuvenation, the freedom enjoined by the Fourth Commandment (Mark 3:1-5; Luke 13:11-17).

Even at the end of His ministry, a few days before He died to pay for the sins of the world, Jesus indicated that the Sabbath command would continue after His death. In prophesying the destruction that was to come on Jerusalem in A.D. 70, Jesus told His followers,
" But pray ye that your flight be not in the winter, neither on the Sabbath day" (Matthew 24:20).

"...rested the Sabbath day according to the commandment" (Luke 23:56).
History reveals that it was because of political and social pressures that the Sabbath was gradually abandoned for Sunday - long after the

time of the Apostles—severe anti-Jewish attitudes developed in the Roman world during the first and second centuries. As acts of repression, the Romans outlawed circumcision, sacrificing, Sabbath keeping and other Jewish practices. Consequently, Christians, particularly at Rome, found it expedient to put as much distance as possible between themselves and the Jews, to demonstrate to the Romans that they were not Jewish.

One way they did this was to work on the Sabbath. Sunday, which was already used by many Romans as a holiday, was a convenient substitute. For a detailed account of this substitution, see the book From Sabbath to Sunday by Samuele Bacchiocchi (Gregorian Pontifical University Press, 1974).

When Constantine officially recognized Christianity in the fourth century, he put the power of the empire behind Sunday observance. In the centuries that followed, the first day of the week became so firmly entrenched as the "Christian Sabbath" that even Protestant reformers could not dislodge it, though they claimed their authority from the Bible and Bible only.

Sunday observance was adopted for the sake of political expedience and is based solely on church tradition. The seventh-day Sabbath, on the other hand, is rooted firmly in the authority of God's Word! Which is your source of authority?

What you need to do is present this to your Bishop or church leader. You are not following the truth, although this may upset the time requires it, too many of our people do not serve God when they assume they do. I asked you to repent and you were offended but you need to. If what I Have stated here is wrong disprove it with the Bible because frankly, I am not concerned with your personal feelings as you expressed above. As you can see my day of worship is according to the bible yours is of the world and this world is of Satan John 14:30

To all of the brothers and sisters who received the truth in this.
Please visit
Join our social network www.truedisciplesofchrist.org
www.tdocrecordings.com
www.kahantazadaq.net

Warning: to homosexuals and Lesbians that claim that they serve Yah (God)
Yahawah (God) does not make anyone gay, yet he shall punish them with death for the act unless they repent. There is no such thing as being born gay it is merely a strong sexual lust. This info is not to condemn anyone with such problems but to move them to alter their mindset. James1:15] "Then when lust hath conceived, it bringeth forth sin :(when a man because a faggot and a woman a freak and lust women they sin by breaking the law see Lev 20:13) and sin, when it is finished, bringeth forth death (the first form of death is spiritual death separation from God)".

Whatever god you homosexuals and lesbians serve it is not the God of the Bible, Romans 1: [26] For this cause God gave them up unto vile affections: for even their women did change the natural use into that which is against nature (this tell us its unnatural for a woman to lay with a woman, so how can you fix your lips and say you were born with the wicked spirit of same-sex lust?) That is a wicked spirit that needs to be cleaned
[27] And likewise, also the men, leaving the natural use of the woman, burned in their lust one toward another; men with men working that which is unseemly, and receiving in themselves that recompense of their error which was meet.

[28] And even as they did not like to retain God in their knowledge, (this is when fem spirit gets on a man and male spirits get on a female and they become confused as to what sex they are because they do not have Yahawah in their thoughts) God gave them over to a reprobate mind, to do those things which are not convenient;" What

is the punishment for such acts under the Old Testament Lev 20: [13] if a man also lie with mankind, as he lieth with a woman, both of them have committed an abomination: they shall surely be put to death; their blood shall be upon them".

Now under the new covenant those brothers and sisters can repent that is where the mercy of Christ comes in. I am not condemning anyone with such problems, but you must repent. You will not enter the congregation as a homosexual. The spirit that is on you right now is of Satan. I am going to reinitiate the spirit of all gays and lesbians is of the devil!! Yahusha Is not a God of confusion, 1st Corin 14: 33] "For God is not the author of confusion, but of peace, as in all churches of the saints".

Further, you fag and lesbians will not enter the kingdom of God unless you repent and live as civilized human beings. And to those that say you are okay as long as you don't bother them, they will be judged by Yahawah as well. Roman 1: 32]" Who knowing the judgment of God, that they which commit such things are worthy of death, not only do the same but have pleasure in them that do them".

1s Corin 6: [9] Know ye not that the unrighteous shall not inherit the kingdom of God? Be not deceived: neither fornicators, nor idolaters, nor adulterers, nor effeminate (men with the spirit of women acting like a woman), nor abusers of themselves with mankind, [10] nor thieves, nor covetous, nor drunkards, nor revilers, nor extortioners, shall inherit the kingdom of God. Because of people as yourself, God destroyed Sodom and Gomorrah Jude 1: 7]" Even as Sodom and Gomorrah, and the cities about them in like manner, giving themselves over to fornication, and going after strange flesh(women for women and men for men and animals), are set forth for an example, suffering the vengeance of eternal fire". 2nd Peter 2: [6]" And turning the cities of Sodom and Gomorrha into ashes condemned them with an overthrow, making them an ensample unto those that after should live ungodlily".

Brothers and sisters with this problem do not deceive yourselves if you do not repent you will be viciously entertained by the sword of Yahawashi (Christ) do not allow your friends to deceive you have to clean yourselves up, repent, and abstain from that wicked, unclean lifestyle. If you are an intelligent human being you should be able to look between your legs and determine which sex you are. Repent for the sword of Christ shall be bathing in the blood of the unclean.

True Repentance

To inherit eternal life in the kingdom of Yahawah established by Yahawashi one must first repent. Despite how righteous you may claim to be you must repent to be accepted into the glorious kingdom. Luke 13: 3] "I tell you, Nay: but, except ye repent, ye shall all likewise perish". The word perish is defined as 1. To die or be destroyed, especially in a violent or untimely manner:

2. To pass from existence; disappear gradually: Sense all have sinned we must all repentant of our former ways and never return to them and we must put on the full armor of Yahawah to avoid sinning. In the book of Ephesians 6:11, the scripture reads "Put on the whole armor of Yah that ye may be able to stand against the wiles of the devil."

What is the scripture speaking about? What does the word armor mean? Armor is all of the tools used to wage a battle or to defend one's self when in battle. The battle spoken of in these next verses is a type of spiritual battle, which has been waged against the people of Yah in this wicked corrupt world. One of the very first things that Yahawashi spoke of when he began to teach was repentance, Matthew 4: [17] "From that time Jesus began to preach and to say, Repent: for the kingdom of heaven is at hand".

The reason that it is essential to repent is because we are all guilty of breaking the laws of Yahawah for to sin is breaking of the law. In other words, if we do not obey or disobey that which Yahawah has commanded we break the law and we are sinning. 1st John 3: 4] "Whosoever committeth sin transgressed also the law: for sin is the transgression of the law".

If you do not study the laws of the Old Testament, then how will you know what sin is? You can not. It is therefore essential that we know the laws. We know that the scriptures are clear to all of those priests blessed by Yahawah.

Before anyone suggests that Christ came to change the law let me refer you to Matthew 5:17 where Yahawashi(Jesus Christ) provides his confirmation that laws are still in effect, Matthew 5: 17] "Think not that I am come to destroy the law, or the prophets: I am not come to destroy, but to fulfill.[18] For verily I say unto you, Till heaven and earth pass, one jot or one tittle shall in no wise pass from the law, till all be fulfilled".

When you sin, you begin to kill yourself spiritually and mentally for when you sin you separate yourself from Yahawah this spiritual death is then followed by a physical death. Romans 6: [23] "For the wages of sin is death, but the gift of God is eternal life through Jesus Christ our Lord". For the sins that we commit, we are rewarded with death in this life and the one that follow if we do not repent. Proverbs 28: [4] "They that forsake the law praise the wicked (when you disobey the laws of Yahawah, you may praise filthy R& B singers, Gangster rappers, women that model semi-nude on billboards signs and TV) but such as keep the law contend with them.

(Yet those of us that keep Yah's laws are content with keeping the laws for we understand the importance thereof)[5] Evil men understand not judgment (if you follow this world you do not truly understand or perhaps disbelieve the judgment of Yahawah) but they that seek the LORD understand all things". To escape condemnation, one must acknowledge his his sins, ask for forgiveness and sin no more. Psalms 51: 3] "For I acknowledge my transgressions: and my sin is ever before me. [4] Against thee, thee only, have I sinned, and done this evil in thy sight: that thou mightest be justified when thou speakest, and be clear when thou judgest". Job 33: 27] "He looketh upon men, and if any say, I have sinned, and perverted that which was right, and it profited me not;[28] He will deliver his soul from going into the pit, and his life shall see the light".

The mistake that many people make is to assume that treating people nicely will get them into heaven. Or they feel that they can change on their own without obeying the law. One cannot change and live in accordance with the laws unless one knows the laws. You have to know it to live but it for this is the sort of change that Yahawah requires of us, Psalms 119: 9] "Wherewithal shall a young man cleanse his way? by taking heed thereto according to thy word".

It is the laws of Yahawah that change us into the Christ-like being of which he intends us to be. Psalms 19: 7] "The law of the LORD is perfect, converting the soul: the testimony of the LORD is sure, making wise the simple". Only if Israelites repent in these lands that we were brought to as slaves will Yahawah forgive us and raise us back up to power. It is following the law that makes one perfect.

2nd Chronicles 6: [36] "If they sin against thee, (for there is no man which sinneth not,) and thou be angry with them, and deliver them over before their enemies, and they carry them away captives unto a land far off or near; [37] Yet if they bethink themselves in the land whither they are carried captive, and turn and pray unto thee in the land of their captivity, saying,

We have sinned, we have done amiss, and have dealt wickedly; [38] If they return to thee with all their heart and with all their soul in the land of their captivity, whither they have carried them captives, and pray toward their land, which thou gavest unto their fathers, and toward the city which thou hast chosen, and toward the house which I have built for thy name".

Once we repent our sins are forgiven and washed away, Acts 3:[19] "Repent ye therefore, and be converted, that your sins may be blotted out, when the times of refreshing shall come from the presence of the Lord"; If you return to that same sin you are worthy of death, Romans 1: [32] "Who knowing the judgment of God, that they which commit such things are worthy of death, not only do the same, but have pleasure in them that do them". Romans 6: [23] "For the wages of sin is death; but the gift of God is eternal life through Jesus Christ our Lord"

The price that you will pay for your sexual wickedness, stealing, cheating, lying, backbiting, mistreating the poor, and disobeying parents is death unless you repent and not return to those ways. Yet if you repent and accept Yahawashi you can be saved, Acts 16: [31] "And they said, Belief on the Lord Jesus Christ, and thou shalt be saved, and thy house".

Yet you, must, you must first repent, Acts 26: 20] "But showed first unto them of Damascus, and at Jerusalem, and throughout all the coasts of Judaea, and then to the Gentiles, that they should repent and turn to God, and do works meet for repentance". Although the laws were only given to the nation of Israel, we have failed to keep them which explains our being enslaved throughout the world today. We are still under Satan's authority. Romans 9: 31] "But Israel, which followed after the law of righteousness, hath not attained to the law of righteousness".

To all Israelites that received this message from the spirit of which it was written.

An Antidote For Aphasia

NOTICE OF DEFAULT IN DISHONOR and ESTOPPEL

Notice to agent is notice to principal and notice to principal is notice to agent.

Date: February 22, 2024,   Certified Mail
#9589071052700481254517

Jacqueline Alisa Smith
Authorized Representative for JACQUELINE A. SMITH and all derivatives thereof.
3567 Creek View Drive, Rex, Georgia [30273]
Jacqueline Alisa Smith
Principal

To: Attention: CFO: Jason Kulas

P.O. Box Irving, TX75016

Hereinafter collectively referred to as RESPONDENT,

Regarding Case Number: 5169264 / ID Number:

Perpetual Claim Number:
70200640000161553136/99589071052700481254524

Greeting Mr. Jason Kulas, I hope this Notice of Default in Dishonor and Estoppel finds you in sound health and good stead.

This is a **Notice of Default in Dishonor and Estoppel** upon the following DEMAND FOR VALIDATION AND PROOF OF CLAIM NOTICE AND RIGHT TO CURE: Certified Mail# 99589071052700481254524

1. **Conditional Acceptance for Value** on or about January 31, 2024, with the U.S.P.S.
   Certified Tracking Number 99589071052700481254524

2. **Notice of Fault and Opportunity to Cure** on or about January 31, 2024, with the U.S.P.S.

   Certified Tracking Number 99589071052700481254524

   Both items show delivered, received, and signed by you or your agent at the address referenced above.

DEFAULT: Your failure to honor the offers places you at **Default**. For your failure, refusal, or neglect in the presentment of verified responses to my Conditional Acceptance for Value and to my **Notice of Fault and Opportunity to Cure**, by you acquiesce you do tacitly agree with all terms, conditions, and stipulations set forth within the Debt Validation **Conditional Acceptance For Value**.

DISHONOR: By the terms and conditions of the agreement resulting from the offer and acceptance of the Conditional Acceptance for Value, you are under the duty and obligation to timely and in good faith protest and/or honor the Debt Validation **Conditional Acceptance For Value**. Your dishonor of the Debt Validation **Conditional Acceptance For Value** discharges the alleged liability that you have claimed.

Allowing twenty-one (21) days for you to respond timely and in good faith protest and/or honor the Debt Validation **Conditional Acceptance for Value**, and an additional ten (10) days on the **Notice of Fault and Opportunity to Cure**, the time allowed is now past for you to in good faith protest and/or honor the Debt Validation **Conditional Acceptance For Value**. As a result, I am showing no record of your response. I now deem the Debt

An Antidote For Aphasia

Validation Conditional **Acceptance For Value** to have been dishonored**,** and the **Notice of Fault and Opportunity to Cure** to have been dishonored**,** thereby comprising a confession of judgment on the merits.

Failure by yourself to respond within the timeframe provided has resulted in the following:

1. You are given the estoppel for your failure to answer back to me of your claim.
2. You are in tacit agreement. No debt or balance is owed for the loan number above.
3. You are possibly under the rule of Jeopardy, and/or fraud as described in 18 U.S. Code CHAPTER 47—FRAUD AND FALSE STATEMENTS.
4. You are Estopped from any further collection activity regarding this matter.

For the account number above, kindly set the balance to zero and mail the clear title to the mailing address above.

Of this Notice and of the included bill, take due **Notice** and heed, and govern yourself accordingly.

Thank you for your prompt attention to this matter.

Sincerely,

_____

Jacqueline Alisa Smith

Authorized Representative For JACQUELINE A. SMITH
All rights reserved

No liability. Errors & Omissions Excepted

An Antidote For Aphasia

WITHOUT PREJUDICE – NON-ASSUMPSIT - Calls may be recorded.

JURAT

IN WITNESS WHEREOF I hereunto set my hand and seal on _____ day of _____ 2024 and hereby certify all the statements made above are true, correct, and complete.

_____

Jacqueline Alisa Smith

State of _____)
                        ss.
County of _____)

Subscribed and sworn to (or affirmed) before me on this _____ Day of _____ 2024.

by _____, (: Jacqueline Alisa Smith proved to me on the basis of satisfactory evidence to be the person who appeared before me.

_____ (seal) Signature

An Antidote For Aphasia

From: Jacqueline Alisa Smith
3567 Creek View Drive
Mail# 99589071052700481254524
Rex, Georgia [30273]
Hereinafter collectively referred to as "Claimant"

Date: January 31, 2024

Certified

To: Attention:
CFO: Jason Kulas
P.O. Box
Irving, TX75016
Hereinafter collectively referred to as RESPONDENT,
CC: Exter Finance
P.O. Box 677
Wilmington, OH, 451-0677

DEMAND FOR VALIDATION AND PROOF OF CLAIM NOTICE AND RIGHT TO CURE

Jason Kulas Chief Financial Officer,

Affidavit is being sent to you in response to a computer generated, unsigned letter dated January 23, 2024, attached here with. In response to your letter, I am conditionally accepting your offer upon proof of claim that you are not at fault for failure to respond to the claimant's first debt validation letter. This is NOT a request for "verification" or proof of Claimant mailing address, but a request for VALIDATION and PROOF OF CLAIM made pursuant to FDCPA (VALIDATION OF DEBT). I respectfully request that your offices provide Claimant with competent evidence as per the attached "Declaration and Proof of Claim" that I have any legal obligation to pay you the unsubstantiated debt. You were previously sent a debt validation letter in the form of an affidavit to which you were required to respond point to point. You failed to validate the debt by responding to each point. You are now at fault for your failure to respond accordingly. This is an opportunity to Cure your Default.

Furthermore, you must cease all verbal communication. No phone calls to the Claimant. Your office now has ten (10) days to produce the required documentation in accordance with FTC guidelines.

It is not now, nor has it ever been, my intention to avoid paying any obligation that is lawfully owed by the Claimant.

If your offices fail to respond to this validation and proof of claim request within ten (10) days from the date of your receipt of this Affidavit, all references to this account must be deleted and completely removed from the Claimant credit file and a copy of such deletion request shall be sent to Claimant immediately. If you fail to respond your acquaintance is consenting that the alleged debt is set off, settled, and closed.

CREDITOR/DEBT COLLECTOR DECLARATION and PROOF OF CLAIM

Provide all the following information and submit the appropriate forms and paperwork back to me along with an Affidavit signed By Title 28 U.S.C. § 1746 within 10 days from the date of your receipt of this request for validation and proof of claim. Your failure to respond to each point herein is a failure to respond and will render you in default. Acquiescence is agreement.

1. Attach a copy of any signed agreement the alleged debtor/claimant has made with the debt collector or other verifiable proof that the debtor/claimant has a contractual obligation to pay the debt collector. Show me that you are licensed to collect in Georgia. Provide me with your license numbers and Registered Agent

2. Furnish a copy of the original promissory note/agreement redacting
my social security number to prevent identity theft and state that your client named above is the holder in due course of the note agreement and will produce the original for my own and a judge's inspection should there be a trial to contest these matters.

3. Produce the account and general ledger statement showing the full

accounting of the alleged obligation that you are now attempting to collect. This is inclusive of; the FR 2046 balance sheet (OMB #'s 2046, 2049, 2099), the 1099 OID report, S-3/A registration statement, 424-B5 prospectus, RC-S & RC-B call schedules – A complete payment history documented from original creditor. This requirement was established by the case – Fields v. Wilber Law Firm, Donald L. Wilber, and Kenneth Wilber, USCA-02-C-0072, 7th Circuit Court, Sept 2004.
4. Verified specifically, the name(s) of the person(s) assigned as Trustee to manage the Corporation's affairs and to be held accountable for the actions of the Corporation. Such as the CFO and subordinates responsible for debt collections.
5. Verify as a third-party debt collector, you have not purchased evidence of the alleged debt and are proceeding with collection activity in the name of the original maker of the note.
6. Verify the stated creditor that you are authorized to act for them.
At this time, I will also inform you that if your offices have reported invalidated information to any of the three major Credit bureaus (Equifax, Experian, or TransUnion) this action might constitute fraud under both Federal and State Laws. Due to this fact, if any negative mark is found on any of my credit reports by your company or the company that you represent, I will not hesitate to bring legal action against you for the following:
Violation of the Fair Credit Reporting Act
Violation of the Fair Debt Collection Practices Act
Defamation of Character

If your offices can provide the proper documentation as requested in the following Declaration, I will require at least 30 days to investigate this information and during such time all collection activity must cease.
Also, during this validation period, if any action is taken that could be considered detrimental to any of my credit reports, I will consult with my legal counsel for suit. This includes listing any information to a credit reporting repository that could be inaccurate or invalidated or verifying an account as accurate when in fact there is no provided

proof that it is.

If your offices fail to respond to this validation request within 10 days from the date of your receipt, all references to this account must be deleted and completely removed from my credit file and a copy of such deletion request shall be sent to me immediately.

I would also like to request, in writing, that no telephone contact be made by your offices to my home or to my place of employment. If your offices attempt telephone communication with me, including but not limited to computer-generated calls and calls or correspondence sent to or with any third parties, it will be considered harassment, and I will have no choice but to file a suit. All future communications with me MUST be done in writing and sent to the address noted in this letter by USPS.
It would be advisable that you assure me that your records are in order before I may be forced to take legal action. This is an attempt to correct your records; any information obtained shall be used for that purpose.

You have ten (10) days from the receipt of this Conditional Acceptance to respond on a point-by-point basis, via affidavit, under your full commercial liability, signing under penalty of perjury that the facts contained therein are true, correct and complete, and not misleading. Mere declarations are an insufficient response. If an extension of time is needed to properly answer, please request it in writing Failure to respond will be deemed agreement with the facts stated in the attached affidavit and an inability to prove you are your claim, thereby indicating your agreement to the facts stipulated herein enclosed commercial affidavit.

This letter constitutes constructive notice to the recipient.
Name _____
Date _____

All responses shall be directed to me, by U.S.P.S Certified or

An Antidote For Aphasia

Registered Mail, at the following address:
Jacqueline Alisa Smith
3567 Creek View Drive   Certified
Mail# 9589071052700481254524
Rex, Georgia [30273]

Service in any other matter will be deemed defective on its face.
State of Georgia
County of Clayton   JURAT
Subscribed and sworn to (or affirmed) before me on this _____ day of _____,
by _____
proved to me based on satisfactory evidence to be the person who appeared before me.

SIGNATURE

PROOF OF SERVICE

I am over the age of 18 and not a party to this action.

I am a resident of or employed in the county where the mailing occurred; my business address is: 190 Janaf Shopping Ctr 23502.

On _____, I served the foregoing document(s) described as: **Flash Drives Social Distancing Covid -19 Debt As A SPC 1099 OID 21 hours , A4V Complete 3 Step Process Webinar over 18 Hours , 1099 OID Process 5 hours DVDs** to the following parties:

**Donald Donaldson
45-645 Pua Alowalo Street
Kaneohe, Hawaii, United States 96744**

[X] (By U.S. Mail) I deposited such envelope in the mail at Norfolk, **Virginia** with postage thereon fully prepaid. I am aware that on the motion of the party served, service is presumed invalid if the postal cancellation date or postage meter date is more than one day after date of deposit for mailing.

[ ] (By Personal Service) I caused such envelope to be delivered by hand via USPS service to the address above;

[ ] (By Facsimile) I served a true and correct copy by facsimile during regular business hours to the number(s) listed above. Said transmission was reported complete and without error.

I declare under penalty of perjury under the laws of the State of Virginia that the foregoing is true and correct.

DATED: _____

NAME OF PERSON MAILING DOCUMENTS

The following Debt Validation was used by Crystal and other to the title to their cars

From: Hereinafter collectively referred to as "Claimant" To: Hereinafter collectively referred to as RESPONDENT, you, your company RE: Alleged account # Certified Mail # NOTICE OF DISPUTE; DEMAND FOR VALIDATION AND PROOF OF CLAIM To Whom it May Concern This letter is being sent to you in response to a computer-generated, unsigned letter dated August 24, 2009 received by Claimant from your offices.

This is NOT a request for "verification" or proof of Claimant's mailing address, but a request for VALIDATION and PROOF OF CLAIM made pursuant to FDCPA (VALIDATION OF DEBT). I respectfully request that your offices provide the Claimant with competent evidence as per the attached "Declaration and Proof of Claim" that I have any legal obligation to pay you the unsubstantiated debt. Furthermore, you should cease all verbal communication.

No phone calls to the Claimant. Your offices have 30 days to produce the required documentation in accordance with FTC guidelines. It is not now, nor has it ever been, my intention to avoid paying any obligation that is lawfully owed by the Claimant. If your offices fail to respond to this validation and proof of claim request within 30 days from the date of your receipt, all references to this account must be deleted and completely removed from Claimant's credit file and a copy of such deletion request shall be sent to the Claimant immediately. CREDITOR/DEBT COLLECTOR DECLARATION and PROOF OF CLAIM Please provide all of the following information and submit the appropriate forms and paperwork back to me along with an Affidavit signed In Accordance with Title 28 U.S.C. § 1746 within 30 days from the date of your receipt of this request for validation and proof of claim.

1. Please attach a copy of any signed agreement the alleged debtor/claimant has made with debt collector or other verifiable proof that the debtor/claimant has a contractual obligation to pay the debt collector.
2. Furnish a copy of the original promissory note/agreement redacting my social security number to prevent identity theft and state that your client named above is the holder in due course of the note agreement and will produce the original for my own and a judge's inspection should there be a trial to contest these matters.

3. Produce the account and general ledger statement showing the full accounting of the alleged obligation that you are now attempting to collect. Such as FR 2046 balance sheet (OMB #'s 2046, 2049, 2099), 1099 OID report, S-3/A registration statement, 424-B5 prospectus, RC-S & RC-B call schedules – A complete payment history documented from original creditor. This requirement was established by the case – Fields v. Wilber Law Firm, Donald L. Wilber and Kenneth Wilber, USCA-02-C-0072, 7th Circuit Court, Sept 2004.

4. Verified specifically, the name(s) of the person(s) assigned as Trustee to handle Corporation affairs and to be held accountable for the actions of the Corporation. Such as the CFO and subordinates responsible for debt collections.

5. Verify as a third-party debt collector, you have not purchased evidence of the alleged debt and are proceeding with collection activity in the name of the original maker of the note. 6. Provide verification from the stated creditor that you are authorized to act for them. Disputing the Debt, Dated this _____ day of _____, . By: _____ (expressly all rights reserved), Real Party in Interest, Live breathing man. Debt Validation & Proof of Claim – 1 of 2 Sending this document using the "Proof of Mail" through the post office is a method some attorneys use, because the recipient is not alerted to possible legal action by the use of a signature card. State of)) ss.: County of) Subscribed and Affirmed and having been duly sworn to at _____ (town/city) before me_____, a Notary Public for the said county and state as above noted, do hereby state that the living man, personally appeared before me and signed the foregoing instrument. Witness my hand and official seal this_____day of_____, 2009. _____ Notary Public Signature _____ My Commission Expires [SEAL] cc:

1. FILE 2. NATIONAL DEFAULT SERVICING 3. DEPARTMENT OF COMMERCE 4. CONSUMER RESPONSE CENTER 5. COUNTY RECORDER

The United States of America)
The State of NEW YORK)SS. DECLARATION OF A LIVING MAN AND PROOF OF IDENTITY,
The County of KINGS) ALLEGIANCE, DOMICILE, AND CLAIM AMERICAN NATIONAL STATUS AND
) BIRTHRIGHT AND ON THE SOIL OF NEW YORK AS IDENTIFICATION
) And HEIR AND BENEFICIARY OF THE PUBLIC TRUST

PICTURE

An Antidote For Aphasia

I, Kahan Tazadaq Shah, a Living Breathing Man of sound mind, of Yamasee/ Hebrew Posterity birthright under Treaty, a sovereign Inhabitant on soil within New York's boundaries, one of the several States as The United States of America, do depose and invoke the People's Laws as Constitution of the United States of America as amended A.D. 1791, Constitution of The State of New York A.D.

1816 and Laws thereof including those of perjury and money, and the Common Law of New York including Due Process of Law, and as a Posterity Beneficiary of the Public Trust formed by said Laws and reserving these same Laws within the same soil Boundaries and without loss of memory or abandonment of the same, and "out of the limits and jurisdiction of the United States", except by constitutional obligations, now speak-Hereafter " I ", or "My". I bind My Conscience, to tell the truth in a certain, complete, and Kahan Tazadaq Shah full manner, by My knowledge, belief, and memory say:

1. I Kahan Tazadaq Shah, the family of Shah, a son of the Almighty Ever Living, and one of the sovereign People of "The United States of America", and an heir and beneficiary of the Constitution thereof as amended A.D. 1791; As a New York, I state and depose for the specific purpose of establishing My valid Claim of sovereignty and sovereign immunity as a matter of Law.

2. This Affidavit is to Amend any previous documents that I may have filed in the public record, or other proceedings, about My linage, or My Claim with regards to My Birthright under Treaty and is intended to correct any errors in those previous documents that I may have mistakenly or inadvertently made. In the event of a conflict between this and any previous documents, the statements and Claims in this Affidavit shall be determined to be My correct Claims on the matter.

3. I hereby Claim My Birth Right and sovereignty as a direct descendant i.e. the posterity, of my people the Yemassee who were a multiethnic confederation of Native Americans who lived in the coastal region of present-day northern coastal Georgia near the Savannah River and later in northeastern Florida Sovereign to this land.

Those people, My direct ancestors, are originals on this land. We were and are the Americans before any Europeans that created and signed the

An Antidote For Aphasia

Declaration of Independence, A.D. 1776; the Articles of Confederation, A.D. 1776; the Constitution of the Commonwealth of Virginia, A.D. 1776; the Constitution for "The United States of America", as amended A.D. 1791; and, also created the several States and "The United States of America", and granted limited powers of their sovereignty to those Nation-States formed thereby.

Further, Yemassee pledged their lives and property to the support and defense of the Constitutions of the newly formed States to which they had granted limited powers of their sovereignty. As the direct posterity of these people, I make My Claim as a beneficiary of the Constitution for "The United States of America", as amended in 1791. I Claim American National sovereignty by inheritance as a principal to, and subject of, the Treaty of Paris, A.D. 1783, as a matter of International Law.

4. Reliance on the pledge of the United States of, in good faith, and having actual knowledge of the facts, authorize, direct, and instruct you, as appointed Fiduciary Trustee, to take the undersigned charges and bonds, including Miller Act Bonds, drawn on KAHAN TAZADAQ SHAH Treasury Direct NO. 123-23-4567. Designees are to "Chargeback" and fully settle (UCC 1-102), and discharge the debt, by presentment of attached bonds to the receiver of the Federal Window (UCC 4-206), or Depository bank (UCC 4-105), and use of my private exemption, exemption number: 123-33-7891 as the principal for the exchange, and charge the Undersigned's..

Deposition of My sovereign Linage recognized by International Law
4. I was born [separated from My Mother] a Living Breathing Free Man and American National [by Birthright] on Month_____. Date_____ Year_____, on the soil of New York, Certified Birth record # 12345678. I Am, and all of My ancestors were, of the Yamasee of Hebrew Israelite Nation. I Am the product of a holy wedlock between Israelite parents, each of whom was heirs and beneficiary, by Birthright passed to them from the
Yamasee sovereign Israelites American People to the Constitution for

"The United States of America", as amended AD. 1791; thereby, endowing Me as an heir and beneficiary of that Constitution by Birthright, and Public Trust Fund Accepting and acknowledging the Oath of office and Corporate

An Antidote For Aphasia

bonds of all officers in his/her official acts as officers, full faith and credit ought to be given in all courts of justice and elsewhere as witnessed herein below.

5. My Father was _____, family of Shah, a Free Man and sovereign [by Birthright] born ____. _____, AD. _____, As Certified on Birth certificate #123456 date filed 12-12-1966, filed on the land Records of the county of New York.
12. My Mother was _____, Family Bynum, a Free Woman and sovereign [by Birthright] born on _____ A.D. _____, As Certified on Birth certificate #123456 date filed 12-12-1966, filed on the land Records of the county of _____.;
Specific Authority for My Claim of Sovereignty as a Matter of Law
13. I am only a sovereign-Inhabitant, in New York, one of The several states of The United States of America, an alien to and "out of the limits and jurisdiction of the United States" with only constitutional obligation of allegiance to said "The United States of America".
14. My photographic likeness and signature is affixed to the upper corner of the first page.
15. My height is approx. five feet and ten inches, weight approx. one hundred and eighty-five pounds, brown hair and black beard, eyes brown, a brown complexion, and Man gender.
16. My political and commercial Status is only on the Soil in that plane within New York one of Our The United States of America, to which permanently I adhere and give allegiance.
17. I, an American national sovereign Inhabitant am domiciled on the soil of New York, Kings county near Township fourteen (14), Range nine (9), Section fifteen (15) and intend to remain within Indiana as per Our Constitution of A.D. 1816 at "Article XL § 17 Boundaries" [as if recited herein in full], these soil Boundaries define the place and plane where I permanently adhere.
18. I will defend, support, and appear In Re: always on the Soil and in that plane within the Boundaries stated as per Constitutions and Laws noticed herein.
22. As an American national sovereign, I reserve the Right to Politically challenge and do not waive, but invoke, the Constitution as Law for new amendments as applied to the Unconstitutional and void, purported 14th amendment to the Constitution of the United States. I do not under invoked Common Law, as aforesaid, waive Due Process of Law.
23. I do not Politically recognize any Constitutional possibility of a non-

several State citizens.

24. My Heavenly Father YHWH has never granted me the authority to animate or make use of an artificial" LEGAL PERSON".

25. Upon My Birthright, moral will, political choice, and treaty, I have previously absolutely and entirely renounced and abjured any deceitful presumptive non-state citizenship whether stated as United States Citizen, citizen of the United States, or other such purported municipal citizen. I reserve the right to amend this Affidavit.

26. I have observed witness #1 full name and second witness full name carefully read and witness this" affidavit: DECLARATION OF A LIVING MAN AND PROOF OF IDENTITY, ALLEGIANCE, DOMICILE, AND CLAIM AMERICAN NATIONAL SOVEREIGN STATUS AND BIRTHRIGHT AND ON THE SOIL OF NEW YORK AS IDENTIFICATION, HEIR, AND BENEFICIARY OF THE PUBLIC TRUST" at this place, plane, and date. Further, I saith not. Done FEB 15th AD 2024

_____

Kahan Tazadaq Shah, Status on the soil as above, Territorial to The United States of America as above.

The United States of America)
The State of New York   )ss. Notary Public Acknowledgement
The County of Kings   )

I, a Notary Public, certify that I know, or have satisfactory evidence that Kahan Tazadaq Shah is the man who appeared before me in relation to New York only on the soil, and acknowledges that he signed his affidavit:: DECLARATION OF A LIVING MAN AND PROOF OF IDENTITY, ALLEGIANCE, DOMICILE, AND CLAIM SOVERIEGN STATUS AND BIRTHRIGHT AND ON THE SOIL OF CALIFORNIA AS IDENTIFICATION, HEIR, AND BENEFICIARY OF THE PUBLIC TRUST" duly witnessed by two people each whose affidavit of witness They and I witness and are attached, and acknowledge it to be his free and voluntary act for the uses and purpose mentioned in the document. Done this 15th day of February A.D.

_____

Notary's Printed Name: Tom Henry Jones, Notary Public in and for the

An Antidote For Aphasia

State of New York. My appointment expires: _____; My county of residence is Los Angeles.

The United States of America)
The State of New York   )ss. Affidavit of First Witness
The County of Kings   )

I, Wendy Smith- First Witness being of lawful age and sound mind, upon the Laws of perjury do depose and say, I aver to tell the truth as I know it to be and provide the following facts to the best of my knowledge and belief. Upon my personal knowledge, belief, and understanding, I state the following to be true, correct accurate, and not misleading:

1. My name is Wendy Smith and live at or near Brooklyn, New York.
2. I have known the Yamasee/Israelite man, Kahan Tazadaq Shah for approximately 6 years and 3 months. On this date of February 16th A.D. 2018, I have personally read and examined a document styled, "Affidavit: DECLARATION OF A LIVING MAN AND PROOF OF IDENTITY, ALLEGIANCE, DOMICILE, AND CLAIM SOVEREIGN STATUS AND BIRTHRIGHT AND ON THE SOIL OF NEW YORK AS IDENTIFICATION, HEIR, AND BENEFICIARY OF THE PUBLIC TRUST" of this date, for Kahan Tazadaq Shah and witnessed his signature thereto and for the purpose indicated state the following.

3. That I believe that the age, Birthright, birthplace, height, weight, gender, hair color, eye color and race are true and correct and not misleading, as indicated on the certificated Birth Record and: affidavit: DECLARATION OF A LIVING MAN AND PROOF OF IDENTITY, ALLEGIANCE, DOMICILE, AND CLAIM SOVERIEGN STATUS AND BIRTHRIGHT AND ON THE SOIL OF NEW YORK AS IDENTIFICATION, HEIR AND BENEFICIARY OF THE PUBLIC TRUST".

4. Further, the photo likeness and signature for Kahan Tazadaq Shah upper left of page 1' of his Affidavit is the proper photo likeness and signature and are true and correct, both as that of Kahan Tazadaq Shah's American National Sovereign Status and Identity done within the jurisdiction and on New York's soil as the place and plane indicated.

5. The signature affixed below the aforesaid photo likeness was made in my presence on the soil as the act of Kahan Tazadaq Shah, and represents his sovereign Status, Identity, Allegiance, and Political union to Indiana de jure, as one of The several States of The United States of America.

6. I believe the Domicile on the soil and Political choice of Kahan Tazadaq Shah as an American national sovereign Inhabitant of New York, one of The United States of America to which he adheres, and his explicit act of having renounced and abjured, on the soil within the place and plane of New York de jure, any deceitful presumptive non-several State citizenships is his true Political choice.

7. On this date and place I have observed Wendy Smith Haase read and witness the aforesaid "Affidavit: DECLARATION OF A LIVING MAN AND PROOF OF IDENTITY, ALLEGIANCE, DOMICILE, AND CLAIM AMERICAN NATIONAL SOVEREIGN STATUS AND BIRTHRIGHT AND ON THE SOIL OF NEW YORK AS IDENTIFICATION, HEIR, AND BENEFICIARY OF THE PUBLIC TRUST".
I Declare, under penalty of perjury, pursuant to the laws of The state of New York and the Laws of The United States of America, that the forgoing is true, correct, not misleading, and I believe accurate, based upon my current knowledge and belief. Freely executed by my hand on February 16th A..D. 2024, at or near Brooklyn, New York.
I

_____

Mark Edmund Wilmes, First Witness.

The United States of America)
The State of New York   )ss. Notary Public Acknowledgement
The County of Kings   )

I, a Notary Public, certify that I know, or have satisfactory evidence that Kahan Tazadaq Shah is the man who appeared before me in relation to New York only on the soil, and acknowledge that he signed his affidavit:: PROOF OF IDENTITY AND EXISTANCE, ALLEGIANCE, DOMICILE AND CLAIM AMERICAN NATIONAL SOVEREIGN

An Antidote For Aphasia

STATUS AND BIRTHRIGHT ON THE SOIL OF NEW YORK IDENTIFICATION" duly witness by two people each whose affidavit of witness They and I witness and are attached, and acknowledge it to be his free and voluntary act for the uses and purpose mentioned in the document. Done this 15th day of February A.D.

_____

Notary's Printed Name: Kahan Tazadaq Shah, Notary Public in and for the State of New York. My appointment expires:_____; My county of residence is Brooklyn.

The United States of America)
The State of New York   )ss. Affidavit of Second Witness
The County of Kings   )

I, Wendy Smith- Second Witness being of lawful age and sound mind, upon the Laws of perjury do depose and say, I aver to tell the truth as I know it to be and provide the following facts to the best of my knowledge and belief. Upon my knowledge, belief, and understanding, I state the following to be true, correct accurate, and not misleading:

8. My name is Wendy Smith and live in or near Los Angeles, California.

9. I have known the white man, Kahan Tazadaq Shah for approximately 6 years and 3 months. On this date of July 16th A.D. 2018, I read and examined a document styled, "Affidavit: DECLARATION OF A LIVING MAN AND PROOF OF IDENTITY, ALLEGIANCE, DOMICILE, AND CLAIM AMERICAN NATIONAL SOVEREIGN STATUS AND BIRTHRIGHT AND ON THE SOIL OF NEW YORK AS IDENTIFICATION, HEIR, AND BENEFICIARY OF THE PUBLIC TRUST" of this date, for Kahan Tazadaq Shah and witnessed his signature thereto and for the purpose indicated state the following.

10. I believe that the age, Birthright, birthplace, height, weight, gender, hair color, eye color, and race are true and correct and not misleading, as indicated on the certificated Birth Record and: affidavit: DECLARATION OF A LIVING MAN AND PROOF OF IDENTITY, ALEGIANCE, DOMICILE AND CLAIM SOVEREIGN STATUS AND BIRTHRIGHT AND ON THE SOIL OF CALIFORNIA AS IDENTIFICATION, HEIR AND BENEFICIARY OF THE PUBLIC TRUST".

11. Further, the photo likeness and signature for Kahan Tazadaq Shah at the

upper left of page 1' of his Affidavit is the proper photo likeness and signature and are true and correct, both as that of Kahan Tazadaq Shah in Sovereign Status and Identity done within the jurisdiction and on New York's soil as the place and plane indicated.

12. The signature affixed below the aforesaid photo likeness was made in my presence on the soil as the act of Kahan Tazadaq S hah, represents his sovereign Status, Identity, Allegiance, and Political union to New York de jure, as one of The several States of The United States of America.

13. I believe the Domicile on the soil and Political choice of Kahan Tazadaq Shah as American national sovereign Inhabitant of Brooklyn, New York, one of The United States of America to which he adheres, and his explicit act of having renounced and abjured, on the soil within the place and plane of New York de jure, any deceitful presumptive non-several State citizenship is his true Political choice.

14. On this date and place I have observed Wendy Smith Haase read and witness the aforesaid "Affidavit: DECLARATION OF A LIVING MAN AND PROOF OF IDENTITY, ALLEGIANCE, DOMICILE AND CLAIM SOVEREIGN STATUS AND BIRTHRIGHT AND ON THE SOIL OF NEW YORK AS IDENTIFICATION, HEIR, AND BENEFICIARY OF THE PUBLIC TRUST".

I Declare, under penalty of perjury, pursuant to the laws of The state of New York and the Laws of The United States of America, that the forgoing is true, correct, not misleading, and I believe accurate, based upon my current knowledge and belief. Freely executed by my hand on February 16th A.. D. 2024, at or near Brooklyn, New York.
I

Mark Edmund Wilmes, First Witness.

The United States of America)
The State of New York   )ss. Notary Public Acknowledgement
The County of Kings   )

I, a Notary Public, certify that I know, or have satisfactory evidence that Kahan Tazadaq Shah is the man who appeared before me in relation to New York only on the soil, and acknowledges that he signed his affidavit:: PROOF OF IDENTITY AND EXISTANCE, ALLEGIANCE,

DOMICILE AND CLAIM AMERICAN NATIONAL SOVEREIGN STATUS AND BIRTHRIGHT ON THE SOIL OF CALIFORNIA AS IDENTIFICATION" duly witnessed by two people each whose affidavit of witness They and I witness and are attached, and acknowledge it to be his free and voluntary act for the uses and purpose mentioned in the document. Done this 15th day of July A.D.

_____

Notary's Printed Name: Tom Henry Jones, Notary Public in and for the State of New York. My appointment expires _____; My county of residence is Brooklyn.

An Antidote For Aphasia

I encourage both brothers and sisters to take heed to the divine Right

Knowledge that the creator has instilled within Kahan Tazadaq that is being dispatched to you from this scroll. Henceforth before you do anything, I encourage you to be quick to listen, slow to speak, and slow to anger. That is James Chapter 1 verse 19. Everything that I say is rooted in the word because I am Yahuah's (God's) man. This divine message is inspired by Yahuah/God, and you have been blessed to receive this Right Knowledge within this manual that will change your life and make you successful.

Humbled thyself and be by Proverbs 18 verse 13, which says he who answers before listing that it is folly and shame. The Bible was written in a masculine form therefore when God uses words like man, he is often referring to women as well. Through the spirit of the Most High in Christ, this book has been strategically designed to align your thinking with the paramount laws of success. As you follow and apply the step-by-step life-altering guides you will begin to discover amazing breakthroughs and new doors of opportunity will open within your life.

Don't give up and your efforts will earn greatness and success. Stop depending on others to get you to the stop. Do the work! One does not become successful by following the trend. One becomes successful by pushing beyond what you have been told was impossible, into greatness. When we examine the word impossible therein is the word possible. Henceforth wherever you hear the aphorism impossible see it as I'm possible because I am. God is within me I 'm possible.

This is the ultimate manual for greatness, motivation, and success that will compel you to observe and change your financial circumstances. Get up and live, stop merely existing. Shalom

An Antidote For Aphasia

ABOUT THE AUTHOR

Kahan Tazadaq is one the most controversial sought-after, Private Banker, Secured Party Creditor, sex educator, dating coach, and relationship expert with millions of YouTube views alongside his books, flash drives, webinars, and seminars coverage across the world. Kahan Tazadaq is also the author of many books on the Redemption process and understanding contracts.

Made in the USA
Columbia, SC
01 July 2024